Country Traditions

TIME-LIFE BOOKS

Alexandria, Virginia

Country Traditions

*preserving America's
rich ethnic heritage*

A REBUS BOOK

CONTENTS

INTRODUCTION

6

In the English Manner

A Hunting Box · A Hunt Breakfast · Tudor Revisited
English Chintz · An Indoor Garden
The English Country House

8

The Flavor of France

Old-World Style · French Provincial Chairs
Rooms with a View · The Pottery of Quimper
A French Twist · French Cottons

46

The Pennsylvania-German Way

Collectors' Choice · Decorative Lehnware · Reviving the Past
Pennsylvania Jacquards · Pennsylvania Flavor
Traditional Soft Pretzels · The Pretzel Basket

78

Scandinavian Tradition

Colorado Mountain House
Carl Larsson's "Ett Hem" · A Norwegian Collection
Norwegian Decorated Trunks

130

Southwestern Style

A Colorful Cottage · Growing Cacti Indoors
In the Pueblo Style · Weathering a Cupboard

150

SELECTED READING

168

CREDITS

170

INDEX

171

ACKNOWLEDGMENTS

175

I nfluenced by history and handcraftsmanship, and incorporating a rich amalgam of regional and ethnic traditions, the American country look draws its inspiration from many cultures, both here and abroad. These traditions may be handed down through generations, as families preserve the heritage—and heirlooms—of their ancestors. Or, they may be adopted after traveling to foreign countries or living in a particular area of this country where the customs of the people who settled there centuries ago still linger.

Located throughout America, the thirteen houses presented on the following pages reflect the influence of five countries and regions whose long-standing cultural traditions lend themselves especially well to country living: England, France, Scandinavia, the American Southwest, and southeastern Pennsylvania, where Germanic immigrants began settling in the late 1600s. In some cases, the distinctive style of the house itself was a starting point for a particular look. For example, the handsome architectural detailing in a Tudor house on Long Island suggested comfortable, overstuffed chairs and Regency pieces that would be in keeping with its stately feeling and also recall the timeless traditions of an English country manor. Similarly, the owners of a Pennsylvania farmhouse were inspired by their historic homestead to begin researching and collecting Pennsylvania-German furniture and folk art; today—thirty years later—the residence remains an impressive testament to their efforts.

In other instances, houses were built by their present owners to capture the flavor of another land. A Colorado couple (one of whom is Danish) wanted a home that would recall the warmth and comfort of houses they had known in Scandinavia. It took them twelve years to complete their Rocky Mountain residence, which includes such touches as exposed beams, raised panels, and elaborate painted and carved decoration, all inspired by traditional Nordic designs. A couple from New Jersey chose to build their oceanside vacation home in the style of barns found in the south of France. By decorating its lofty, beamed interior with traditional French country furniture and accessories, they have managed to re-create the romantic spirit of Provence.

But while every house in this book has a strong regional or ethnic feeling, each one also derives much of its character from the individual tastes and interests of its owners. Indeed, few of the homeowners were purists about creating a particular look, and many of them chose to combine traditional furnishings with pieces they already owned. A Pennsylvania hutch can be found next to a French farm table, Chinese porcelain and Spode stone china are displayed side by side, and Mexican weavings share a room with Navajo rugs. Drawing inspiration from another time or place, these handsome interiors demonstrate the range of looks that can all be part of country style.

In the English Manner

the pleasures of English country life

Achieved with an uninhibited mix of color and pattern, eclectic furnishings, and a profusion of accessories, the English country look is one of timeless comfort. Leather sofas, chintz-covered easy chairs, botanical prints, and needlepoint pillows all have a place in handsome rooms that seem to have evolved unconsciously over many generations. The effect is friendly and hospitable, evoking the ease of life in the English countryside.

Each of the houses in this chapter has borrowed a different element from English style. The decor of one was inspired by the owners' interests in such longtime English pursuits as fox hunting and carriage driving. The look of a second, a vacation home used often for entertaining, draws on the convivial feeling of the English country house. And finally, a weekend getaway for two amateur gardeners pays tribute to the English love of nature by bringing the outdoors in with pretty floral-motif furnishings.

Colorful chintz fabrics and comfortable armchairs create an inviting sitting area.

A Hunting Box

Located in the hunt country of southeastern Pennsylvania, the restored 1700s fieldstone farmhouse above has been renovated and decorated to reflect a passion for fox hunting and carriage driving. The residence is part of an eight-acre complex that also includes a refurbished stone barn, a recently built pole barn, and a paddock, right, which currently accommodates ten horses. A country place such as this would be known in England as a "hunting box"—an 18th-century term for a rural retreat that a sportsman who lived in town would maintain as a base for "riding to hounds."

Although the property was in a state of disrepair when the present owners found it—the yard was overgrown, the house had been neglected for many years, and the barn roof was near collapse—renovating it provided the couple with a welcome opportunity to integrate home and hobby. The large stone barn now houses stables, as well as a collection of antique carriages and sleighs that are driven both for pleasure and in horse shows and coaching competitions along the eastern seaboard. The residence, which retains its original pine woodwork and stone fireplaces, has become a cozy headquarters for

Continued

Begun around 1740, the Pennsylvania fieldstone house above was enlarged later in the century.
Horses used for fox hunting and carriage driving are turned out from their stables to the fenced paddock,
right; in bad weather, they find shelter in the adjacent pole barn.

Above, an 1842 English engraving of a road coach hangs over the original mantelpiece in the drawing room.

the various hunting and driving activities enjoyed by the homeowners.

The decor of the house followed no particular plan, but instead evolved hand in hand with the interests of the owners, to whom a relaxed atmosphere was especially important. "We want our home to be an extension of our casual lifestyle, not a showcase," say the couple, who frequently host traditional hunt breakfasts during the fall-to-winter fox hunting season, as well as gatherings after carriage drives.

Much of this entertaining takes place in their

handsome hunt room, which was originally the keeping room of the circa 1740 house. Informal and comfortable, the space is furnished with Oriental rugs and a mix of antiques and re-productions, from both England and America, which have been acquired gradually over the years. The English country look that prevails in the hunt room, and throughout the rest of the house, derives in part from this furniture, which includes a number of Queen Anne- and Chip-pendale-style pieces in rich, dark woods, some with leather upholstery. The homeowners' ex-

Continued

The dining room, above, features a Queen Anne-style table and chairs and a 19th-century cherry side-board.

13

The collection of hunting and carriage-driving artwork in the hunt room, at left, features a 19th-century French bronze horse, set atop an English refectory table. The curved mahogany table is known as a hunt desk; such pieces have been used since the 1700s in England and America, both as desks and as sideboards for serving hunt breakfasts.

The silver fox head above is
a contemporary English
version of the stirrup cup,
traditionally used to serve
spirits to mounted riders
before a hunt. While the fox
"mask" is the most common
design, other popular motifs
include boar's heads and the
heads of hunting dogs.

tensive collection of sporting art and related accouterments, however, also makes an important contribution to the overall effect.

Over time, the collection, which began with an 1842 English engraving of a road coach, has expanded to include a broad range of prints, oil and watercolor paintings, bronze and silver sculptures, canes, and boxes, all featuring designs that are based on hunting and driving themes. Reflecting Britain's obsession with horses and related equestrian pursuits, such pieces were particularly popular with the English gentry in the 18th and 19th centuries.

Interspersed among these artworks are articles of the couple's own riding attire, as well as horns, whips, and other accessories they them-

Continued

Garments used for hunting and driving are stored in the livery room cupboards, above, along with ribbons and mementos from sporting events.

Articles of formal hunting attire are displayed in the hunt room, opposite—except when the owners are "riding to hounds." Tradition and etiquette dictate that a gentleman wear a scarlet jacket, a black top hat, and russet-topped black boots; a lady rider wears a black jacket, derby, and boots.

The sleigh above is a Portland Cutter, made around 1910 in Kalamazoo, Michigan. On the barn walls are lead bars used to join two pairs of horses; the black leather harnesses are for formal occasions.

selves use for fox hunting and for driving their fifteen meticulously restored English and North American sleighs and carriages. The horse-drawn carriages date from the 1890s to around 1910, and were intended as sporting vehicles. The star of this remarkable collection is their 1898 Park Drag; essentially a sophisticated version of a stagecoach, the elegant carriage was designed for park driving, going to the races, and for country picnics—a role it still serves admirably today.

The Park Drag, right, is a sporting carriage built by the London coachworks of J. A. Lawton in 1898. Here, it is being readied for a drive, along with one of the four horses needed to draw it.

A HUNT BREAKFAST

Meant to revive fox hunters after an invigorating ride—or to fortify them beforehand—the hunt breakfast has been associated with riding to hounds ever since the early days of the sport in the 1700s.

This hearty meal was originally based on the traditional English gentleman's breakfast, typically a sumptuous spread of meats, game, fish, eggs, cheese, baked goods, and fruit.

No one menu is standard for the hunt breakfast, which actually can be served at any time of day, however, and the foods and beverages could vary. The English, for example, often include a kidney dish, or fish such as haddock or the smoked herring known as kippers. Americans, in turn, might lean toward their own domestic specialties—Virginia ham, perhaps, or cornbread or sweet potatoes.

Planned for a party of eight, the menu presented here is ideal for serving buffet-style, as is currently done by many hunt clubs in the United States. It offers some traditional hunt breakfast foods, and can easily be adapted to suit individual tastes. You may, for example, want to serve a different type of cheese than the strong-flavored Stilton that is suggested, or replace the toast with biscuits or rolls—perhaps the soft Scottish breakfast rolls known as "baps." Recipes for scrambled eggs, pan-fried potatoes, grilled tomatoes, blueberry-ginger scones, and lemon-almond pound cake follow; use your own favorite recipe for the baked country ham.

· MENU ·

Baked Country Ham

Dilled Scrambled Eggs with Smoked Salmon

Pan-Fried Potatoes with Scallions

Grilled Basil Tomatoes · Blueberry-Ginger Scones

Toast with Assorted Jams and Marmalade

Lemon-Almond Pound Cake

Strawberries with Whipped Cream · Stilton

Nuts and Dried Fruits

Fresh Orange Juice · Champagne

Tea and Coffee

◆

DILLED SCRAMBLED EGGS WITH SMOKED SALMON

12 eggs
1/3 cup water
1/4 cup chopped fresh dill,
    or 1 tablespoon plus
    1 teaspoon dried

1/2 teaspoon pepper
5 tablespoons butter
1 large onion, finely chopped
6 ounces smoked salmon,
    thinly sliced

    1. In a large bowl, beat the eggs, water, dill, and pepper; set aside.
    2. In a large skillet, heat 3 tablespoons of the butter over medium heat. Add the onion, and cook, stirring, until translucent, about 5 minutes.
    3. Add the remaining 2 tablespoons butter, and when it melts, add the egg mixture. Cut the salmon into bite-size pieces and scatter them over the eggs. Cook the eggs over medium-high heat until firm but still moist, 4 to 5 minutes, using a whisk or fork to stir the eggs up from the bottom of the pan. Serve immediately.   8 servings

◆

PAN-FRIED POTATOES WITH SCALLIONS

2 pounds small red potatoes,
    unpeeled
3 to 5 tablespoons butter
3 to 5 tablespoons oil

3 garlic cloves, minced
1 bunch scallions, coarsely
    chopped
Salt and pepper to taste

    1. Wash the potatoes and place in a large saucepan; add water to cover. Bring the water to a boil, reduce to a simmer, and cook the potatoes until barely tender, 10 to 15 minutes. Drain and set aside to cool slightly.
    2. Cut the potatoes into 1/2-inch slices.
    3. In a 12-inch skillet, preferably nonstick, melt 1 tablespoon of the butter in 1 tablespoon of the oil over medium heat. Add the garlic and the scallions, and sauté until softened, about 5 minutes. Remove the garlic and scallions from the pan and set aside.
    4. Add 2 tablespoons of butter and 2 tablespoons of oil to the pan juices, then add the potatoes in a single layer. Cook the potatoes, turning them frequently, until golden, 13 to 15 minutes. Add more butter and oil as necessary during cooking. Stir in the reserved scallions and garlic.
    5. Transfer the potatoes to a serving dish. Sprinkle with salt and pepper, and serve.   8 servings

◆

GRILLED BASIL TOMATOES

6 tablespoons grated Parmesan
    cheese
2 teaspoons dried basil

1 teaspoon pepper
16 plum tomatoes

    1. Preheat the broiler. Line a baking sheet with foil.
    2. In a small bowl, stir together the cheese, basil, and pepper.
    3. Cut a thin slice from both ends of each tomato. Stand the tomatoes on the prepared baking sheet and sprinkle about 1 teaspoon of the cheese mixture on top of each tomato.
    4. Broil the tomatoes 4 inches from the heat until the topping is just golden, 3 to 5 minutes. Watch carefully; the topping can brown very quickly.
    5. Arrange the tomatoes on a platter and serve immediately.

        8 servings

Tableware with a sporting or nature theme is an appropriate complement to a hunt breakfast. In the setting above, the hot dishes are served on a plate depicting a whimsical chase scene, while a blueberry scone is framed by a ribbon of greenery on an ivy-motif butter plate. Cut-glass jam cups and a silver toast rack are elegant accessories.

BLUEBERRY-GINGER SCONES

4 cups flour
¼ cup sugar
3 teaspoons ground ginger
2½ teaspoons baking powder
1 teaspoon salt
2 teaspoons grated orange zest

4 eggs, lightly beaten
⅔ cup heavy cream
1 stick (4 ounces) chilled butter,
    cut into pieces
2 cups fresh blueberries

1. Preheat the oven to 400°. Lightly grease two large baking sheets.

2. In a large bowl, stir together the flour, sugar, ginger, baking powder, and salt. Stir in the orange zest.

3. In a small bowl, stir together the eggs and the cream; set aside.

4. Using a pastry blender or two knives, cut the butter into the dry ingredients until the mixture becomes coarse crumbs. Make a well in the center.

5. Pour in the egg mixture and stir just until blended. Add the blueberries and continue stirring gently until the mixture forms a dough that can be gathered into a ball; do not overmix.

6. Divide the dough in half. On a lightly floured surface, pat out one portion of dough to a 1-inch-thick round, 7 inches in diameter. Repeat with the remaining dough.

7. Using a sharp knife dipped in flour, cut each round of dough into 6 wedges. Transfer the wedges to the prepared baking sheets. Bake until the scones are puffed and golden brown, 15 to 20 minutes. Serve hot.

Makes 1 dozen

◆

LEMON-ALMOND POUND CAKE

¾ cup sliced almonds
3 cups flour
½ teaspoon baking soda
¼ teaspoon salt
2 sticks (8 ounces) butter, softened
    to room temperature
2 cups granulated sugar

4 eggs
1¼ teaspoons lemon extract
2 tablespoons lemon juice
1 tablespoon grated lemon zest
1 cup buttermilk, or 1 cup milk
    plus 1 tablespoon vinegar
2 tablespoons confectioners' sugar

1. Preheat the oven to 350°. Butter and flour a 10-inch Bundt pan.

2. Place the almonds in a dry skillet and toast them over medium heat, stirring often, until lightly browned, about 7 minutes. Set aside to cool to room temperature.

3. In a medium bowl, stir together the flour, baking soda, and salt; set aside.

4. In a large bowl, cream the butter until light. Gradually add the granulated sugar and beat until well blended. Beat in the eggs, one at a time. Then beat in the lemon extract, lemon juice, and zest. Alternating between the two, gradually add the dry ingredients and the buttermilk, beating well after each addition. Fold in the almonds.

5. Spread the batter evenly in the prepared pan. Rap the pan once or twice on the counter to remove any air pockets. Bake until the top of the cake springs back when touched, and a toothpick inserted in the center of the cake comes out clean and dry, 50 to 60 minutes.

6. Let the cake cool in the pan on a rack for 10 minutes, then turn it out onto the rack to cool completely. Sprinkle the top of the cake with the confectioners' sugar.

Makes one 10-inch cake

While "dessert" at a breakfast may seem unusual, sweet foods are welcome before or after a day of riding. The fresh strawberries with whipped cream, dried fruits, nuts, and lemon-almond pound cake above make a light and delightful final course.

Tudor Revisited

This stately brick house, built in a seaside village on Long Island, has been remodeled by a large family that enjoys entertaining throughout the year. Dating to the early 1900s, the eighteen-room vacation residence features a flowing layout that attracted the current owners because it could easily accommodate gatherings of any size. The well-designed renovation not only opened up the interior to more light, but also introduced an English country decor that plays off the Tudor-style architecture of the house.

In planning the project, the owners chose to highlight the building's distinctive Tudor elements, which include diamond-paned leaded-glass windows, ornate ceilings, and the massive fireplace in the living room, while adding new features where appropriate. Dark woodwork was stripped and lightened, and elaborate plaster ceiling moldings restored. New French doors, some with a diamond-paned design, bring in sunlight and offer views of the extensive gardens on the property.

The furnishings, in turn, are well-suited to the

Continued

Whitewash was used to lighten the brick house above, which was built on Long Island around 1913 from a design loosely based on the Tudor style. The library, right, retains the original molded plaster ceiling; the caned armchair and the coffee table are Regency pieces.

Inspired by the rich colors of the Oriental rug, the decor in the living room, left, was designed to hold its own in a space where such architectural features as the ornate ceiling moldings and fireplace surround have a strong presence. Tapestry-like fabrics and oversize chairs are complemented by Chinese porcelains, as well as a collection of 19th-century Spode stone china displayed in a faux-bamboo breakfront.

handsome backdrop the house itself provides. Throughout the rooms, the patterned slipcovers and upholstery, carpets, draperies, and wall-papers—often with bold floral motifs in bright colors—were combined for the rich, layered look that is characteristic of English country-house style. Eight different patterns appear in the living room alone, and even more may be found in the main guest bedroom.

Also rich in variety is the furniture that fills the spacious rooms. These pieces are not limited to any one period or type. "We wanted the house to look as it might have originally, but still incor-porate a mix of styles," says the designer who oversaw the project. "That gives it the feeling of

Continued

Chinese ginger jars and a
pair of colorful porcelain
parrots create an imagina-
tive vignette on the Regency
mahogany sideboard above.
The still-life painting was
done in Italy earlier
in this century.

Conceived as a bright, comfortable room for
entertaining, the dining room, left, is furnished
with upholstered chairs and a large
Chippendale-style table.

*A simple blue and white
scheme was chosen for the
master bedroom, above. The
small 19th-century chaise
is English.*

a country house in England, where such a residence generally would be kept in one family, with the decor evolving piece by piece over the course of many generations."

In addition to early-19th-century tables in the refined, neoclassical Regency style, a number of comfortable Victorian club chairs—covered with new fabric—may be found, as well as pieces in the angular Arts and Crafts style that came into vogue at the turn of the century. Many of these furnishings were chosen for their strong character, in keeping with the generous proportions of the rooms. In the expansive living room, small groupings have been arranged to create

intimate and inviting seating areas, and to break up the space.

Although the decor has a relaxed, unstudied look, that effect was not achieved without considerable effort and meticulous planning. The project, in fact, took two years to complete, and it draws much of its success from a careful attention to the finishing touches. Even the accessories, which include Oriental and English porcelains, needlepoint throw pillows, and colorful botanical prints, were selected with the overall look in mind; as intended, they do much to tie together the various elements of the imaginative English-inspired decor.

Intended to be the most feminine room in the house, the main guest room, above, is enlivened with patterns and frills.

Each guest room has its own distinct style. In the bedroom at right, a "masculine" mood was expressed with autumnal colors and dark wood furnishings such as the turn-of-the-century beds and the marble-topped Empire table. Floral-motif fabrics and colorful quilts soften the look.

The English pressed-glass compote above is an example of Vaseline glass, so named for its liquid appearance and yellow-green color, the result of adding uranium to the glass mixture. This type of glass was introduced around 1840 in Bohemia, and was used for tablewares throughout the second half of the century in America and Europe.

ENGLISH CHINTZ

If any single decorating element could be considered the hallmark of English country style, it is probably chintz. This versatile fabric—a glazed cotton, usually in brightly colored patterns—has a long history in England as a descendant of *chitta,* the printed or hand-colored (and sometimes glazed) cottons from India that first appeared in British ports in the early 1600s. Cool and lightweight, the fabrics, whose bright animal, bird, and floral patterns were colorfast, created a sensation in 17th-century England, where nothing quite like them had ever been seen before.

To take advantage of a ready market, traders began to suggest to the Indian makers specific patterns that would appeal to English buyers; many of these were floral motifs inspired by European botanical prints. The rage for the imported goods led English textile makers to undertake their own production around 1700, and they wisely continued to print their fabrics with the flower patterns the consumers had come to favor. Domestic manufacture expanded as mechanized printing processes developed later in the century, and especially when analine dyes were invented in the 1850s.

Today, chintz remains as popular as ever, with more than a thousand patterns available. Particularly favored are nature-inspired motifs like those on the English chintzes at right, all of which are based on traditional designs.

An Indoor Garden

A vine-covered trellis forms a leafy screen for the porch, above, furnished with vintage wicker.

Aunifying floral theme sets an informal tone for the English country decor of this sunny Long Island house, where the fabrics, wallpapers, and accessories were chosen to create the sense of a rambling garden transplanted indoors. "There are large annual and perennial beds with lots of multicolored flowers on the property, and I tried to capture their spirit," says one of the owners, who is a designer. "We didn't find the architecture of the house that compelling," she adds, "so we concentrated instead on bringing interest to the

rooms through brightly patterned furnishings."

The look of well-established comfort that distinguishes the residence belies the fact that it was necessary to decorate the vacation house—the family's first—virtually from scratch. Remarkably, the entire project was completed in less than six months' time. To accomplish this monumental task, the owners, who are confirmed Anglophiles, acquired many of their furnishings on a single trip to London. "I'd been shopping in the city for years, so I knew exactly which stores to visit," says the designer. "I man-

Continued

A marbleized "tile" pattern was devised for the foyer, above, where the original wood floor remains.

aged to fill an entire ship's container without any trouble." Among its contents were an assortment of wardrobes, twelve chests of drawers, a number of kitchen chairs, some two dozen Staffordshire figurines—and one or two mantels. A few faux-bamboo pieces caught her imagination, but for the most part she opted for plain English pine furniture that she knew she could

Continued

The late-19th-century secretary above is one of several simple pine pieces that were purchased in England and later embellished with painted decoration.

In the living room, left, glazed walls and a pickled floor provide a subdued background for colorful chintz and cotton damask fabrics.

Whimsical hand-painted decoration appears on a bedroom door, as well as on the throw pillows arranged on the bed. The canine portrait was inspired by the work of George Stubbs, a noted 18th-century English sporting artist.

dress up later with decorative paint finishes.

To do so, the homeowners enlisted the help of a professional artist—and good friend—who transformed the pine furnishings with whimsical trompe l'oeil scenes. The artist's work is also evident on a folding screen in the living room, decorated with framed botanical prints, as well as on numerous hand-painted pillows and lampshades. A rich variety of finishes may also be found in various rooms, where surfaces have been glazed, combed, marbleized, and pickled, to create an interesting backdrop that is well-suited to the spirited furnishings.

Colorful hat boxes, botanical prints, and an armoire painted with a trompe l'oeil garden scene accent the floral theme in the sitting room, right.

Floral wallpapers, chintz fabrics, and two vintage quilts in the Grandmother's Flower Garden pattern brighten the cozy third-floor guest bedroom at right. An antique Staffordshire figurine topped with a hand-painted shade serves as the base for the bedside lamp.

The jug above is an example
of Prattware, a type of lead-
glazed earthenware first
made by William Pratt of
Staffordshire around 1785,
and produced until the
1840s. The most common
forms are molded jugs,
which often feature pastoral
scenes rendered in relief.
Colors were typically applied
with green, blue, and brown
underglazing.

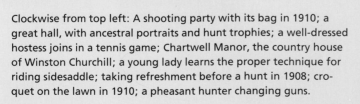

Clockwise from top left: A shooting party with its bag in 1910; a great hall, with ancestral portraits and hunt trophies; a well-dressed hostess joins in a tennis game; Chartwell Manor, the country house of Winston Churchill; a young lady learns the proper technique for riding sidesaddle; taking refreshment before a hunt in 1908; croquet on the lawn in 1910; a pheasant hunter changing guns.

THE ENGLISH COUNTRY HOUSE

The large estate with landscaped grounds known rather simply as the "country house" has a long tradition in England. Descendants of the medieval feudal manor, such rural retreats first became fashionable in the 1600s. At that time, however, the estates were more symbols of wealth than real homes, and were only occupied a few months of the year. It was not until the early 1800s that the country house started to become an important part of English life.

The reasons for this were twofold. In the 19th century, access to rural areas began to increase as roads were improved and railroad lines installed. The new emphasis on family life that emerged during Queen Victoria's reign (from 1837 to 1901) was also having a widespread effect, and the country house became a place where families would get together throughout much of the year.

Social events were a high priority. At eagerly anticipated weekend house parties, guests enjoyed fishing, shooting, and fox hunting. Games of tennis and croquet were played, and children could often be found on horseback or romping with pets. Indoors, where small armies of servants catered to every need, there were lavish balls in the great hall, prodigious meals, and parlor games. Gentlemen gathered in smoking and billiard rooms, while ladies met in the drawing room for tea, conversation, and letter writing.

The Flavor of France

*an adaptable blend
of rusticity and romance*

The French country look has long been a favorite in America. Bespeaking grace and comfort, the style has its roots in Provence in the south of France, known for its sunny climate, charming farmhouses and cottages, and the rich colors of its landscape.

The traditional furnishings of this region, which have changed very little in design since the 18th century, have a simple, robust beauty that is easy to live with today. They are also surprisingly versatile: solid, carved fruitwood furniture, crisp cotton-print fabrics, chunky, hand-thrown pottery pieces, and homey objects such as farm baskets and antique copper cookware all look as handsome in contemporary settings as they do in early houses. And, as the homes on the following pages reveal, such furnishings can be used either to create a completely French look, or simply to accent a decor with a few romantic French country touches.

A trompe l'oeil wall painting suggests a French country pantry.

Old-World Style

*In a corner of the living
room, a circa 1780 Pennsylvania tall-case clock made
of inlaid walnut stands next
to a primitive French ladder-
back armchair dating to
around 1750.*

The owners of this 1779 farmhouse have
long been avid antiques collectors. But
since the couple and their family moved
into their historic Pennsylvania home, that pas-
time has taken a new direction. Most notably,
the emphasis of their collection, once focused
on American country furnishings, has shifted
to pieces of French and other European origins.
That change came gradually as objects were acquired one at a time; yet while the homeown-

Continued

*The living room, right, features a 1770s French
walnut day bed. The whitewashed ceiling and walls
contribute to the French country look.*

ers initially had no definite decorating scheme in mind, the resulting interior has a cohesive look, unified by a distinctly French character.

In large part, the family's new interest in French antiques was inspired by the 18th-century home itself. Many of the interior features, such as the recessed windows, low painted-wood ceilings, and massive mantelpieces, evoke European farmhouses, while also lending the rooms a look of simple elegance. "We can use furniture here that would never have worked in the newer house we lived in previously," one of the owners says. "This house has a distinct ambience; it seemed to call for a richer, more formal

Continued

A small-print wallpaper in the dining room recalls traditional Provençal fabrics. Country French
antiques include the sturdy 1830s farm table and late-19th-century walnut chairs, left,
and the old-fashioned laundry cart, above.

Lanterns, a candlebox, an old hunting horn, and a stuffing spoon are arranged on the window ledge above, while antique tools and wooden pickle tongs are set out on the chest.

country style than anything we had ever lived with before. The curving lines and carving that are characteristic of French country furniture had just the right look."

In furnishing the house, the couple did not start from scratch by replacing all their old pieces. Instead, as they talked to dealers, learned more about European antiques, and discovered objects that appealed to them both, they introduced new finds in ways that seemed appropriate to individual rooms.

Throughout much of the house, the French furnishings are mixed comfortably with locally made antiques that the family have owned for years. In the dining room, for example, an 1830s French walnut farm table has been paired with a handsome 1825 Pennsylvania walnut hutch. And in the original keeping room—which with its walk-in fireplace has an early American look

Continued

The original brick-and-stone keeping room fireplace at left has two ovens; it is surrounded by a display of farm tools, hunting equipment, and cookware.

The Impressionist painting on the wall above suggested the color scheme for this guest bedroom. A romantic mix of floral patterns and ruffles enhances the old-fashioned French feeling.

—the couple opted for such distinctly American furnishings as the ladder-back rocker and iron cookware, and added no French touches at all.

Yet, while all the pieces do not come from France, an old-world French feeling was nevertheless achieved throughout the house with the effective use of accessories, such as 19th-century landscape paintings and antique porcelain. Fabrics and wall coverings were also carefully cho-

sen: elegant silks and damasks distinguish the living room, while small-print fabrics reminiscent of the traditional hand-blocked cottons of Provence, or romantic 19th-century-style wallpapers patterned with bouquets, ribbons, and bows, appear in other rooms. The final effect is a handsome backdrop for comfortable furnishings that look as though they had been part of this farmhouse setting for many generations.

A family member painted the whimsical decoration on the guest room fireplace, opposite, using the floral-print wallpaper as inspiration. Although it is new, the elegant white wicker furniture captures the spirit of the French art nouveau style, which was popular at the turn of the century. Simple swags caught at the corners with bows dress up the windows.

Delicate ceramics have had a prominent place in French interiors ever since the first porcelain factories opened in France in the late 1600s. The hand-painted figurine above, made in the 1830s, is an example of "soft-paste" porcelain, one of the earliest types of ceramics produced in France. For soft paste, clay was mixed with ground glass to imitate the translucent look of more expensive Chinese porcelain.

FRENCH PROVINCIAL CHAIRS

One piece of furniture found in virtually all traditional French country houses is the rush-seated, open-back chair known as a *chaise à capucine*. Taking its name from the simple, sturdy chairs that furnished monks' cells in 16th-century French Capuchin monasteries, this practical seating type has remained popular ever since it was first adopted for household use in the early 17th century.

At that time, most provincial houses were furnished sparsely, with a few rustic pieces of no particular style. By the end of the century, however, rural furniture makers—and their customers—had become more

aware of urban trends, and country furniture soon mirrored fashions found in Paris, albeit in a conservative way.

The austere *chaise à capucine,* with its long tradition of use, was re-worked using new designs, reflected primarily by changes in the back and legs. In the early 1700s, the *chaise* had straight slats and heavily turned legs; by mid-century, wavy slats and more delicate turnings had appeared; by the end of the 1700s, classical lyre and shield motifs formed the backs, while the legs became simple and tapered. The designs have never lost favor, and variations continue to be made today.

Rooms with a View

When they set out to build a vacation house, the owners of this New Jersey shoreline property had a specific goal in mind: they wanted a casual place that would be easy to maintain, but that would still be gracious enough for dinner parties and for entertaining weekend guests. With the help of a designer, the couple achieved just the balance of rusticity and elegance they were looking for. They chose an architectural style inspired by the barns that the designer had admired in the south of France—but with plenty of windows to capture the ocean views. They then decided to furnish the spacious, beamed interior with French furniture, and a range of accessories, including farm tools and earthenware, all characterized by a country look.

The furniture for the house had to be carefully chosen and integrated, since the living, dining, and kitchen areas are all incorporated into a single lofty space, or what the homeowners call their "great room." Fortunately, such traditional French country pieces as farm-kitchen tables, linen cupboards, and armoires proved sizable enough to look well-proportioned in the large area. *Continued*

A collection of farm tools above the fireplace, left, and an arrangement of faience on a rustic table, above, contribute to the casual country French feeling in the living room of this seaside house. The upholstery fabrics were inspired by pretty, provincial prints.

The rush-seated chairs and lattice-door cupboard in the dining area, above, are new, but display styles long favored in southern France.

Moreover, the country furniture, made of walnut or of fruitwood such as pear, was well-suited to the natural setting of ocean, sky, and dunes, and to the straightforward interior finishes—whitewashed walls and oak flooring. The graceful detailing of the French-inspired tables and chairs, the owners have found, also lends a great deal of flair and character to the decor. Although simple and sturdily built, the pieces do not feel primitive, and are easily paired with furniture upholstered in floral fabrics, which add a romantic element to the overall look.

In traditional country French fashion, handsome copper cooking pots, baskets, and glazed pottery are displayed in the kitchen, opposite, where hand-painted cupboards provide plenty of storage. The sunny space opens into the living room.

The unusual headboard in the master bedroom, right, was custom-made from antique floorboards. The painted decoration recalls flower and dove motifs from Provençal folk art.

THE POTTERY OF QUIMPER

In the mid-16th century, craftsmen from Faenza, Italy, introduced to France the techniques for making the tin-glazed earthenware known to the French as faience. Faience potteries, or *faienceries,* would flourish in France until the late 18th century, when economic problems forced most of them to close.

Among the potteries that did survive—and that continue to produce faience today—were several in the town of Quimper (pronounced cam-pair) in Brittany. Unlike the more fashionable *faienceries,* which were producing fancy tablewares for the rich, the Quimper workshops made bowls, plates, pitchers, and other utilitarian items that served the everyday needs of the locals. It was because these wares were so useful and inexpensive that the Quimper potteries thrived while others failed.

Initially, all Quimper pieces were simply decorated, often with just a transparent glaze, but during the 1700s, as potters from areas with more sophisticated workshops began to settle in the town, the decoration became more elaborate and pictorial. It was not until about 1860, however, that the Quimper potters, in an effort to cater to the tourist trade, began decorating their pieces (which now included souvenir items such as snuffboxes, knife rests, and place card holders) with quaint, provincial motifs. It is these charming designs, shown on the late-19th- and early-20th-century pieces at left, that have come to distinguish Quimper and that remain popular today.

A French Twist

This remarkable house overlooking the Atlantic Ocean on eastern Long Island was dubbed with the name "Poky Hall" by its present owner, a designer and accomplished trompe l'oeil painter, when he purchased the property. At the time, the residence certainly lived up to its name; painted gray throughout, it was a poky little 1930s cottage, with low ceilings

Continued

Sponge-painted walls set off a collection of 18th-century Dutch delft pottery, above. The delft platter inset in the mirror inspired the painted decoration on the frame.

The "summer room," left, features a variety of French country seating pieces covered in provincial fabrics. The "delft" chandelier is the result of a skilled hand at trompe l'oeil painting.

A wall was taken down between two small rooms to create the large, sunny living room at right, which displays a paneled mantel and chimney piece designed and painted by the homeowner. The French chairs and tables date to the 1700s, and the curtain fabric is a reproduction of an 18th-century French linen.

Faience—brightly colored, decorated tin-glazed earthenware—has been made in France since the 16th century, and is widely collected today. Among the most sought-after pieces are ornamental dishes, such as the early-19th-century example above, that were made complete with an assortment of trompe l'oeil fruits, nuts, and vegetables.

and small windows. "I didn't love the building, but the location was beautiful," recalls the designer, who originally planned to stay just long enough to fix up the property as an investment. As he worked, however, he became inextricably involved with the cottage, and in fact has lived there ever since—all the while transforming it into a handsome "French" farmhouse.

A French look, however, was not the original idea; when he first moved in, the owner fur-nished the residence with American antiques and bright chintzes. But as business began taking him to France twice a year, he decided he was ready for a change, and started the gradual shift to a country French decor. Well-established in the design field, he already had a solid knowledge of French antiques, and his travels to the south of France increased the possibilities for locating the sort of formal but comfortable furnishings to which he is drawn.   *Continued*

French linen in a brown-and-white plaid was used to cover the walls of the dining room, above. The cupboard, from southern France, holds 19th-century faience, as well as Staffordshire and majolica pieces.

A gilded papier-mâché dog lies patiently next to a ficus tree in the front entryway, opposite. The trompe l'oeil pattern on the floor—which visually connects the hall area to the dining room beyond—was designed and hand-painted by the homeowner to create the look of ceramic tiles that have become worn with age and use.

Soon after the designer began acquiring French pieces, his American furniture disappeared into storage. The house is now filled with tables, chairs, desks, and armoires from France that date from the 17th through the 19th centuries. In particular, he looked for pieces that still had their old painted finishes intact, and for unusual chairs that retained their original upholstery. Where new upholstery was called for, he used the florals and stripes, and the blue-and-white and brown-and-white checks, that are traditional to country French decor.

The collections, however, are by no means

Continued

Staffordshire sheep vases and a horse figurine, above, add to the pastoral look of the green-and-white bedroom. The table lamp was also made from a Staffordshire figure.

Unified by a strong floral theme, the bedroom at left has an English look that sets it apart from the French-inspired decor of the rest of the house.

73

A reproduction of a Louis XV printed linen was used for the wallcovering, upholstery, bedspread, curtains, and valance in the sunny bedroom above.

limited to furniture alone. Designed to catch and delight the eye, imaginative groupings of artworks and accessories—antique engravings, faience and delftware pieces, carved busts and statuettes, and even a few straw hats—appear in every room.

Perhaps even more intriguing, however, are the tromp l'oeil designs, all originated and painted by the designer himself, that distinguish the house. With considerable skill he has "replaced" old wood floors by convincingly replicating stone and tile floors of the kind typically found in French farmhouses. Walls, in turn, have been "paneled" with trompe l'oeil boards or sponged to look like stucco, and mantelpieces "refaced" with marble. The owner's inventiveness with paint has introduced a lively sense of fun to the cottage while enriching it with textures and old-world details that create an appropriate setting for the period French furnishings.

Seating pieces in the bedroom include an 18th-century chaise à dossier en médaillon, *or oval-back chair, opposite. The upholstered easy chair is known as a* bergère.

Throughout Europe in the 18th and early 19th centuries, illustrations of exotic flora and fauna were produced as hand-colored prints that could later be bound into books as a series. The engraving above, entitled "La Piegrieche à plastron blanc" (white-breasted shrike), is one of a number published in Paris by François Levaillant between 1796 and 1812 and included in a volume called The Natural History of African Birds.

FRENCH
COTTONS

Cottons have played a colorful role in France ever since the 1660s, when brightly patterned fabrics from India began being imported there in quantity. As in England, the success of the Indian cottons—known in France as *indiennes*—was dramatic, and domestic textile manufacturers were soon producing their own block-printed versions. As the craze for *indiennes* eclipsed the market for silk and wool, however, many established French textile firms were forced to close. Between 1686 and 1756, some eighty governmental decrees were issued banning both the importation of printed Indian cottons and the domestic production of imitations.

Infractions were punishable by fines, imprisonment, and even death; in some cases, cotton clothing was torn off the backs of wearers. Despite the deterrents, however, or perhaps because of them, the popularity of the *indiennes*—which were smuggled into the country or produced illicitly in clandestine factories—continued. The laws relaxed only in the mid-1700s when France began importing raw cotton from India, offering workers the opportunity to both weave and print the fabric.

While printing with copper rollers has replaced the hand-block method, the industry continues in France to this day. Many of the new fabric designs, like those at right, remain faithful to the early patterns, featuring small florals and paisleys in rich colors inspired by the French countryside.

The Pennsylvania-German Way

a regional style with
Germanic roots

Between the 1680s and the mid-1700s, more than seventy-five thousand Germanic immigrants settled in southeastern Pennsylvania, establishing a distinctive cultural heritage there that is strongly felt to this day. The houses they built for themselves were practical and tidy, their furnishings sturdy and utilitarian—yet both were often enlivened with bright decoration, revealing a love of color that has proved enduring in its appeal.

The three Pennsylvania houses presented in this chapter are all homes to serious collectors who have spent years searching for fine examples of regional furniture and folk art. Here you will find classic Germanic furniture forms, such as the imposing wardrobe known as a *schrank,* as well as locally made pottery, textiles, and frakturs—the beautiful illuminated manuscripts that were the specialty of skilled calligraphers. Each piece alone is a testimony to fine craftsmanship; assembled, they evoke the spirit of Pennsylvania-German artisanry.

A grain-painted Pennsylvania cupboard holds local redware made primarily in the 1800s.

Collectors' Choice

During the three decades they have lived in this rambling house, the owners have filled it with a collection of Pennsylvania furniture and folk art as remarkable for its quality as for its immediate appeal. The color and whimsy of the quilts, whirligigs, paintings, and furniture displayed throughout the rooms contribute to a look of casual charm that belies the uncompromising eye affecting each choice. That eye, in fact, was developed through years of practice, by collectors who—through an intelligent course of study—have gathered pieces that

The handsome house at left, built near Philadelphia in 1934, was designed to recall the historic farmsteads of the region.

not only are superior in craftsmanship, but also work well with their home and lifestyle.

"I didn't intend to collect antiques," says one homeowner, recalling her early taste for contemporary furnishings. Yet, once she found herself interested in early American pieces, she became completely absorbed. In order to build a solid background in an area new to her, she began assembling an extensive reference library, enrolled in classes, and visited museums and private collections before making any major purchases. The time was well spent, as she is now able to recog-

Continued

The living room, right, is the most formal room in the house, and the only one that does not contain any painted furniture. The tall-case clock is the work of George Hoff, a German clockmaker who settled in Lancaster, Pennsylvania, in 1765, and worked there until his retirement in 1806.

Young German women often kept treasured belongings in "brides' boxes"—customarily received from their betrothed at the time of their engagements—and the practice was continued by settlers in America. The late-18th-century Pennsylvania box above was made with a bentwood construction and painted with a traditional Germanic tulip motif.

nize the work of well-known craftsmen and to spot an original finish, an attribute of old pieces she considers especially important. "Doing your homework is the best advice I can pass on," she says. "I still go to museums to compare styles and techniques and to study how authenticated pieces were made before buying objects that are similar."

Her education continued when the couple moved to their present residence from a smaller farmhouse and found that many of their New England antiques seemed lost in its larger rooms.

Continued

In the kitchen doorway, above, stands an unusual Pennsylvania cupboard with its original painted decoration. Whirligigs and a tin squirrel cage are part of the folk-art collection in the dining room, right. The three frakturs were all done by Henrich Otto, who worked in Lancaster County.

"I discovered quickly that furniture has to suit the scale of a house," the homeowner recalls. As a result, she began looking specifically for Pennsylvania-German pieces, which tend to be large and solid in appearance. Her collection now represents many of the classic regional forms; these include the large wardrobe known as the *schrank,* which would hold the clothing of an entire family, and the painted blanket chest, traditionally used for linens.

Among her favorite pieces, however, are the many distinctive hand-lettered and illustrated documents—birth certificates, family registers,

Continued

Designed to stand in the middle of a room, the 19th-century "marriage bed" in the guest room at left has painted decoration on both sides of the head and foot boards.

Much of the blown glass above was crafted in Pennsylvania and New Jersey in the late 18th and early 19th centuries. The enameled bottles and beakers on the center shelf, however, were made in Germany, probably as presentation pieces for special occasions.

Pennsylvania textiles in the bedroom at left include a mid-1800s quilt signed "Lizzie Herr" and a late-19th-century hooked rug.

Birds—painted on the back of a chair, carved as toys, and detailed in a small watercolor—set a whimsical theme, above.

house blessings, bookplates, and love tokens— known as frakturs. Included among these is the work of the highly regarded Pennsylvania artisan Henrich Otto, an ornamental painter who also operated a printing shop in Ephrata in the late 1700s. Otto embellished his fraktur with both hand-painted decoration and block printing; he is noted particularly for his expressive interpretations of flowers, wreaths, leafy vines, and parrots—familiar motifs that today remain hallmarks of the Pennsylvania-German tradition.

The appliquéd quilts at right, made for two sisters, display the same fabrics but different designs. The frakturs on the wall date from the 1800s to the early 1900s.

DECORATIVE
LEHNWARE

Born in 1798, Joseph Lehn was a farmer and cooper of German descent from Lancaster County, Pennsylvania, who gained renown for the decorated woodenware he produced late in life. Around 1860, Lehn turned to woodworking as a hobby. His first pieces were made as gifts, but he was soon offering a broad range of products for sale. These included buckets, kegs, penny banks, game boards, egg cups, trinket cups, sugar tubs, sewing boxes, dower chests, and the small turned lidded boxes used to store saffron, a spice commonly used in Pennsylvania-German cooking.

The craftsman did a brisk trade out of a shop behind his house, near Clay, and also provided his wares to stores in New Ephrata and in Lititz. Purchased as souvenirs and gifts, the pieces were especially popular among visitors to Linden Hall Seminary, a nearby boarding school.

Now known as Lehnware, the decorative wooden pieces can often be recognized by a red-ocher or pale pink background color. Some are grain-painted, and many feature simple stenciled decorations, usually flowers, strawberries, or an abstract vine pattern. Decals of floral sprays and female portraits also appear on some of the later wares, made in the 1880s at about the time the woodworker's eyesight began failing. Lehn stopped making his pieces sometime during that decade and died in 1892; his work, however, continued to be popular, and is sought after by collectors today.

Reviving
the Past

The Pennsylvania home above consists of a 1760s log house moved to the site, and a stone "summer kitchen" built with salvaged materials— including two-hundred-year-old clay roofing tiles.

Passers-by often pause to take a look at this remarkable complex of buildings arranged around an old-fashioned raised-bed garden. Even on a rural Pennsylvania road it is a rare sight, resembling a historic farmhouse— complete with all its outbuildings—that managed to survive intact for two hundred years.

Yet, despite its appearance, the farmstead was actually assembled relatively recently by a couple who wished to create an appropriate setting for their extensive collection of Pennsylvania-German furnishings. Only the 1760s log house, moved to the site from another location, existed

previously. The attached stone "summer kitchen," which contains a sitting area, a kitchen, and a second-floor bedroom, and the small, separate buildings grouped around the yard were all put together from a variety of materials salvaged from 18th- and 19th-century structures. While the outbuildings appear to be traditional farm structures, they in fact serve as a painting studio, a potting shed, and a tool storeroom.

The couple spent ten years building the complex, beginning construction only after much research. Whenever possible, they examined and photographed surviving 18th-century buildings

located in the area, and also studied early tax records, probate inventories, and atlases. Finally, individual craftsmen were hired for each phase of the work.

The goal was not to re-create any one historic building or farmstead, but instead to establish a setting that drew on a variety of historical precedents. The couple now refer to the completed project as a "colonial Federal Revival homestead" because it incorporates both log buildings—the most common type found on Pennsylvania farms prior to 1800—and stone buildings of the sort that would have been add-

ed to a farmstead by second-generation owners.

Dominating the carefully planned complex is the two-story log house, which, built by a German miller, was originally quite plain. In 1790, however, it was bought by an English settler who, during the two succeeding years, made many fashionable improvements: walls and ceilings were plastered, decorative trim was added to the front-hall stairs, and paneling, chair rails, and cornice moldings were installed in the "best rooms."

In reconstructing the house after it was moved to their property, the homeowners kept most of

Continued

Designed to resemble early Pennsylvania-German outbuildings, the two log structures above house a painting studio and a potting shed; the small stone building, modeled after an 18th-century smokehouse, is used for tool storage.

The simple squared-log walls in the kitchen, right, date to 1760, when the structure was built by German settlers; the trim on the stairs was added around 1790 by a subsequent owner.

The 18th-century corner cupboard at left, filled with spatterware, is from Berks County. The distinctive decoration is known as gouge carving, a technique often seen on mantelpieces, but seldom on furniture. The peacock-feather "duster" hanging next to the cupboard, once used to keep flies away from food, is known as a "mich wisch."

When the log house was built, the "stove room," or schtubb, *contained a five-plate stove; a Franklin fireplace like the one above was added in the early 1790s, when the room was "updated."*

these "English" alterations. The general character of the historic log residence, however—its layout and the overall scale of the rooms—remains that of a typical colonial Pennsylvania-German dwelling. On the first floor, for example, the basic three-room plan, which was designed with a kitchen on one side of the central chimney, and a corner bedroom and a "stove room," or *schtubb*, on the other, has been retained. While the original kitchen is now used as a dining room, the other two rooms are furnished

Continued

A Lancaster County schrank *inlaid with pewter dominates the stove room, right. The 18th-century splay-legged plank chairs, also called back-stools, are Moravian pieces.*

Based on historic prototypes, the fireplace in the summer kitchen, above, measures over ten feet wide. The floor pavers were salvaged from a brick walkway.

as they would have been in the late 1700s.

What may have been a family's best pieces—a Lancaster County *schrank* and a leather-uphol-stered armchair—are, for instance, placed in the *schtubb*. This room, the traditional parlor of the German farmhouse, took its name from the stove customarily used for heat. With typical German practicality, the backless five-plate stove would open through the wall into the kitchen fireplace, so that burning wood coals could be shoveled in from the kitchen side—eliminating smoke in the parlor. The square *schtubb* was the most formal room of the Pennsylvania-German farmhouse, and was used to receive honored guests such as the local minister, who would perform weddings and baptisms there.

Continued

The breakfast area, opposite, features a rare broken-arch schrank *from Christiana, Pennsylvania, made around 1740. The heavy twisted column between the doors is a particularly unusual feature, seldom found on such wardrobes.*

Pennsylvania-German tinsmiths flourished in the 19th century, supplying a widespread clientele with everything from lanterns and candle molds to cookie cutters and tea caddies. Relatively inexpensive, tin products were usually left plain, but some, like the circa 1840 coffeepot above, had elaborate punched decoration.

Pennsylvania was rich in iron, and its Germanic settlers proved to be skillful blacksmiths. Most of the objects they produced were utilitarian, such as the double-ended roasting forks and spatulas above.

The original kitchen in the log house is today used as a dining room, left. The primitive hanging cupboard, one of the earliest furnishings in the house, dates to around 1730. Centered over the fireplace is an 18th-century winged head, an image of Saint Sophia. Such pieces were occasionally hung on the exterior of Pennsylvania-German buildings to protect against misfortune.

The rose motif bed coverlets above were woven by John Brosey in Manheim, Pennsylvania, in 1841 and 1842.

While the couple have put considerable thought into furnishing this room, and others throughout the house, they are quick to point out they were not trying to create a documentary interior. "By eighteenth-century Pennsylvania-German standards our house is overfurnished," they say. "But we did try to avoid some excesses, and to keep in mind how things were used." Such "overfurnishing" would have been difficult to prevent given the sheer scope of their collection, which includes Pennsylvania pottery, baskets, wrought-iron pieces, textiles, and furniture,

gathered individually over a thirty-year period.

Remarkable for its variety, the collection is also enriched by historical documentation; in many cases, the homeowners have been fortunate to determine the precise provenance of their pieces. A vibrant grain-painted *schrank* from the Oley Valley in Berks County, for example, is known to have been made in 1775, for one Philip De Turk, by an itinerant artisan who specialized in decorative painting. Some of the chairs, in turn, were the work of Moravians; these religious separatists, who founded a colony

Continued

Painted Pennsylvania furniture in the bedroom, above, includes a grain-painted schrank, *made for Philip De Turk in 1775.*

in Bethlehem, Pennsylvania, in 1740, were widely known for the high quality of their craftsmanship. The collection is further distinguished by a number of items with decorative features such as gouge carving and pewter inlay, rarely found in Pennsylvania-German antiques.

All of these pieces are shown to advantage in the rather plain settings, which, seemingly devoid of 20th-century intrusions, evoke the traditions of another time. The effect, of course, draws its success from the couple's unusual approach. "Most people adapt their collections to suit their surroundings," they say. "We wanted to create an environment to suit our collection."

The 19th-century rope beds in the guest room, left and above, came from different sources but are similar in style. The 1854 friendship quilts, from Rapho township in Lancaster County, however, are a pair; both display dozens of signatures, penned by the men and women who made the individual squares.

*The whitewashed stone
basement, left, is used for
drying herbs and flowers.
Here, a collection of antique
splint-woven and coiled rye
baskets is on display.*

Pennsylvania Jacquards

Trained in guilds, German weavers were highly skilled, and the immigrants who settled in Pennsylvania established a long-standing tradition of superior textile crafting in the region. Among the notable Pennsylvania-German woven pieces are jacquard coverlets like those at right, named for a special loom attachment that was introduced to America from France in the 1820s. Widely used until the Civil War era, the jacquard attachment relied on sets of punched cards to create a predetermined pattern, and made possible far more complicated designs than could be produced previously. A large, complex, and delicately balanced mechanism, it was used only by professional weavers, most of whom were men.

While jacquard coverlets were made and sold throughout the country, Pennsylvania-German pieces are distinctive for their bands of vivid colors and traditional Germanic patterns. Crafted with inexpensive cotton yarn obtained from commercial mills and with homespun wool, the coverlets often feature stripes of three to five different colors worked into the background. Favored motifs, sometimes repeated in blocks, include eagles, tulips, roses, stars, and the distilfink, a traditional Germanic bird design. Unlike New York and New England coverlets, Pennsylvania-German jacquards also typically had fringe on both sides and on the bottom end.

Pennsylvania Flavor

With its fieldstone façade and paneled shutters, the 1804 house above is typical of the early homesteads built by Germanic farmers in Pennsylvania.

This handsome stone farmstead is home to a long-time collector of Pennsylvania-German antiques who was only ten years old when he started to attend auctions and country sales in eastern Pennsylvania. Having lived in the area all his life, he knew instinctively even at an early age that he wanted to learn about and acquire objects that had been made and used locally. At the time, his buying power was limited to an allowance of a dollar a week, but in the 1950s a dollar still enabled him to purchase small items, such as slip-decorated redware pie plates, tin cookie cutters, and carved wood butter prints.

By the time he was in college, he had assembled a fairly sizable selection of pottery, tin,

woodenware, and other household objects. And, after he was married, the collection grew larger still, to include grain-painted cupboards, tester beds, trestle tables, and decorated Windsor chairs, as well as numerous small country items, such as baskets and toleware. "When we bought this old homestead," the collector says, "we came from a little house to a large one, but we still had no trouble filling the new place with all of the things we owned."

For him, moving into the house held particular meaning, as the property had captured his imagination ever since he had first seen it some fifteen years earlier. Quite remarkably, as it turned out, the 1804 farmstead had been erected by his own ancestors, Swiss Mennonites who

Continued

The tiny stone bank house above, the first dwelling on the property, was built in the 1700s; it stands over a spring that still supplies the household with water.

An antique woven rag carpet runs up the center-hall stairway at right. Frakturs, a star-shaped quilting template, and two narrow hooked rugs—which once covered stair treads—help to make up the decorative wall grouping.

had settled in the area in the 1700s. With its stately stone façade, simple, classical entrance, double-hung sash windows, and end chimneys, the central-hallway structure is typical of the Federal-style houses customarily built in the region by successful farmers.

What makes the property unusual, however, is that the first dwelling built on the farm, a tiny stone house that dates to the mid-18th century, still stands just behind the 1804 residence. As was characteristic of many early Germanic farmhouses in the area, the little "bank house" was

Continued

The parlor, above, retains its original gouge-carved fireplace; this is the only carved mantel in the house.

Among the antique utensils displayed in the dining room are a slaw cutter, by the fireplace, and a breadboard, on the mantel. Both are 18th-century pieces.

built into a hillside directly over a spring that provided a continuous supply of cold water to a spring room inside, where perishable foods could be refrigerated. When the larger residence was built, the then outmoded 18th-century bank house was evidently kept for use as an outbuilding.

For someone so devoted to the history and artifacts of the region, this property was an exceptional find. Yet, by the time the couple had

purchased it, the farmstead was considerably run down. In spite of its poor condition, however, the new owners were pleased to discover that virtually all the original details—floorboards, mantelpieces, and folding fireplace shutters—had remained intact.

They also found some idiosyncrasies. In a wing added to the house in the 1830s, for example, there were two kitchens, located side by side. It is probable that when this addition was

Continued

In the dining room, opposite, 19th-century English ironstone in the "Morning Glory" pattern is used to set the collapsible trestle table. Both the early-18th-century table and the late-18th-century cupboard were handcrafted in Lehigh County. The cupboard, or "dresser," features an inset shelf, where pies were traditionally placed to cool.

A regional specialty, shoofly pie was once a familiar sight on Pennsylvania-German tables, and no well-stocked kitchen was without a sturdy plate to bake one in. Decorated with green and brown glazes, the handsome redware pie plate above is attributed to the Dry pottery works of Berks County, and dates to the mid-1800s.

The kitchen, right, features a fireplace with folding doors. Such doors, distinctive to early Pennsylvania homes, were closed to prevent drafts when the hearth was not in use. The large smoke-decorated container on the floor is a flour canister.

The 19th-century painted apothecary chest at left was purchased off the porch of a rural general store in Berks County. Locally made kitchen wares, including decorated stoneware, butter prints, and splint baskets, now fill its shelves.

constructed, the home was divided into separate living quarters for different generations of the same family. At the time, it was not uncommon for a widowed parent to move into one part of a house, while a son or daughter raised his or her own children in another.

With certain modifications, the rather unconventional floor plan of the house proved easily adaptable to contemporary living. The homeowners renovated one of the two old kitchens as a dining room and kept the other as a kitchen. The parlor, traditionally known as the stove

Continued

The grain-painted cupboard above contains several rare examples of Pennsylvania redware; pieces like the 19th-century lion were meant to imitate imported Staffordshire figurines.

Among the Pennsylvania folk-art pieces in the stove room, left, are a 19th-century rocking horse and a tulip-decorated blanket chest.

Small decorative watercolors like those above were done in the Pennsylvania-German tradition of fraktur, but without calligraphy. The bird tree composition, top, was painted by David Herr in 1820, and the parrot design, bottom, was done around 1800 by Henrich Otto; both artists worked in Lancaster County.

room, is now a comfortable family room. Since there no longer was a stove in the house when the couple moved in, they made a point of looking for a suitable old piece, finally locating an early-19th-century example that had been made in Lehigh County. Some time later, while they were working outside, the pair came across part of the original cast-iron stove, buried in the yard. As if in testimony to the appropriateness of their replacement, its design turned out to be a near match to that of the antique they had already purchased.

The decorated blanket chest above, dated 1782, holds a display of storage boxes. The bird tree was made by "Schtochschnitzler," or "cane carver," Simmons, a Pennsylvania craftsman who worked in the late 1800s and early 1900s.

Inset with calico patchwork, the striking chintz quilt in the master bedroom, left, was made in Lehigh County in the 1830s; the linen press, from Berks County, dates to the same period.

A mid-19th-century appliquéd Rose of Sharon quilt brings color to the guest room, right. Both the quilt and the bed, with its unusual turned posts, were made in Lehigh County. The pine corner cupboard dates to around 1800.

Coiled rye-straw baskets like the one above were extremely common in 19th-century Pennsylvania. The baskets, made in numerous shapes and sizes, were practical for food storage, since rodents would not eat rye straw.

TRADITIONAL SOFT PRETZELS

Long associated with the culture of the Pennsylvania Germans, the soft pretzel is a simple yeast bread believed to have been originated by monks in southern France or northern Italy sometime before the sixth century. Legend has it that scraps of dough were twisted into treats for children who recited their prayers properly; the familiar knotted shape, which has passed down through the centuries unchanged, is said to resemble arms crossed in prayer.

The word "pretzel" may in fact derive from the Latin word *brachiola,* meaning "little arms," or the Latin *pretiola,* which translates as "little gifts."

The tradition of baking pretzels eventually spread across the Alps to the Germanic countries of central Europe, where a salty version was favored as an accompaniment for the yeasty beers of the region.

Introduced by European settlers to colonial Pennsylvania, pretzels have remained an important component of the Pennsylvania-German baker's repertoire ever since. They are still made with the same basic ingredients —flour, yeast, water, and salt. Perhaps the only difference is that today's pretzels are frequently dried for crispness after baking.

The recipe opposite is for traditional soft pretzels. These taste particularly good with beer; a spicy mustard and sharp cheese also bring out their flavor.

A. For each pretzel, a piece of dough is rolled into a rope about 19 inches long and a scant ½ inch thick.

B. The rope of dough is shaped into a curve, then the ends are twisted around each other once.

C. After the twist is completed, the ends of the dough are laid on the resulting loop and pressed into place.

D. The baked pretzels are brushed with egg white and sprinkled with coarse salt, then returned briefly to the oven.

SOFT PRETZELS

1⅓ cups lukewarm (105° to 115°) water	1 tablespoon olive oil
1 package active dry yeast	2 tablespoons baking soda
3 teaspoons sugar	1 egg white
About 4 cups flour	About 1 tablespoon coarse (kosher) salt
¾ teaspoon table salt	

1. Place ⅓ cup of the water in a small bowl and sprinkle the yeast over it. Stir in ½ teaspoon sugar and let the mixture stand until the yeast begins to foam, about 5 minutes.

2. In a large bowl, stir together the remaining 1 cup water, 1 cup of the flour, and the table salt, and beat with an electric mixer until smooth, about 1 minute. Pour in the yeast mixture and the oil, then add 2¾ cups flour and mix until well blended.

3. Transfer the dough to a lightly floured surface and knead it until smooth and elastic, about 5 minutes, adding more flour if necessary to prevent sticking. Form the dough into a ball and place it in a large bowl. Cover the bowl with a slightly damp kitchen towel, set it aside in a warm, draft-free place, and let the dough rise until doubled in bulk, about 45 minutes.

4. Punch the dough down, then transfer it to a lightly floured surface. Divide the dough into 12 equal pieces and cover them with a damp kitchen towel. To shape a pretzel, roll out a piece of dough into a rope about 19 inches long and a scant ½ inch thick (Illustration A). Holding the ends, shape the rope into a curve, then twist the ends around each other once (Illustration B). Lay the ends on the resulting loop of dough (Illustration C), and press. Repeat for the remaining dough. Leave the finished pretzels on the floured surface and let them rise, uncovered, until almost doubled in bulk, about 30 minutes.

5. Preheat the oven to 450°. Lightly grease and flour two baking sheets.

6. In a large skillet, bring 2½ quarts of water to a boil over high heat. Add the baking soda and the remaining 2½ teaspoons sugar. Reduce the heat and keep the water at a simmer. Using a slotted spatula, slide 3 pretzels carefully into the water and cook for 20 seconds, spooning the simmering water over them as they cook. Using the spatula, lift the pretzels out of the water, letting them drain for a moment before transferring them to one of the prepared baking sheets. Repeat for the remaining pretzels.

7. Bake the pretzels for about 13 minutes, or until light brown. Remove the pretzels from the oven and leave them on the baking pans. In a small bowl, beat the egg white. Lightly brush the tops of the pretzels with the egg white, then sprinkle each pretzel with coarse salt (Illustration D). Return the pretzels to the oven and bake an additional 2 minutes to set the salt.

Makes 1 dozen

TIPS

◆ Be sure to bake the pretzels *before* glazing and adding the salt; otherwise, they will shrivel.

◆ Because soft, salted pretzels readily absorb moisture, they should be eaten soon after they are made. Any uneaten pretzels can be wrapped in tinfoil and stored in the freezer.

THE PRETZEL BASKET

While pretzels were made in Pennsylvania as early as the 1730s, it was not until 1861 that the first commercial pretzel bakery was opened there. Located in Lititz, it was owned by a baker of Swiss-German descent named Julius Sturgis. Sturgis is said to have obtained his recipe from Ambrose Rauch, a local baker who had reportedly gotten it from a tramp passing through town.

The Sturgis Bretzel Bakery ("bretzel" is the local dialect spelling of pretzel) soon faced competition from scores of other bakeries in Lancaster and Berks counties. These firms turned out hand-twisted pretzels at an average rate of ten pretzels per person per minute. Production increased in 1933, when a company in Reading devised a machine that could "tie" 120 pretzels per minute.

As business thrived, southeastern Pennsylvania became known as the Pretzel Basket, and the industry is still centered there today. Since the pretzel was such a part of life in the area, it was only natural that it would become a mascot of sorts for local groups. One band of musicians who played around Lititz named themselves the Pretzelets. And each year since 1951, a benefit football game—the Pretzel Bowl—has been held, featuring a pretzel-decorated trophy, a parade with pretzel floats, and, of course, a pretzel queen.

Clockwise from top left: N. D. Sturgis, son of Julius Sturgis who founded the first commercial pretzel bakery in America, shown here in the early 1900s; Sturgis bakery employees around the turn of the century; pretzels being shaped and left to rise before baking; a pretzel bakers' float at a Pretzel Bowl parade; Lewis Sturgis kneading pretzel dough in a traditional dough box in the mid-1900s; a pretzel-dispensing robot at a trade fair; a pretzel trophy being presented at a Pretzel Bowl game; pretzels emerging from an automated twisting machine; a Pretzel Bowl Queen on her float; the Pretzelets.

Scandinavian Tradition

*Nordic craftsmanship
and charm*

Scandinavian style reflects a love of home and a respect for handcraftsmanship—two deep-seated sentiments that are linked to the harsh Nordic climate. For centuries, the cold, dark winters forced rural families indoors for months on end, and it was natural that interiors and their furnishings became the focus of attention. The result was a distinctive tradition of Scandinavian decorative arts, including painting, carving, and weaving, that is still strong today.

That same tradition marks the two houses in this chapter, both owned by families with Scandinavian roots. The first, a mountain residence in Colorado, features interiors and furniture decorated with floral motifs adapted from designs used in the centuries-old Norwegian painting technique of *rosemaling*. The second, a rustic cabin in Wisconsin, is filled with a fine collection of handmade Norwegian and Norwegian-immigrant furnishings, including a number of painted chests from the region of Telemark.

Built in traditional Scandinavian style, an oak alcove bed features ornate carving.

Colorado Mountain House

This handsome house in the mountains of Colorado was single-handedly built and furnished by one of the owners to remind his Danish wife of her homeland. While contemporary in feeling—with open spaces, bare floors, and plenty of large windows overlooking the Rockies—it also incorporates many traditional Nordic touches. Among them are the elaborate carved and painted decoration on the interior walls and woodwork, and the handmade Scandinavian-style furniture that has been crafted for many of the rooms.

The original design for the Colorado house at left called for a stucco exterior and a thatched roof, in the style of 15th-century Danish houses. When the town zoning committee vetoed that idea, the homeowners compromised by building a more conventional mountain home, with cedar siding. The cedar-shake roof is steeply pitched to shed snow.

From the time they decided to build the house, the homeowners knew they did not want much outside help, whether it was in drawing the floor plans or erecting the walls. Just five months after the construction started, the couple and their three children moved into the shell of their new residence, prepared to endure living with drywall and plywood until they could afford to decorate each room exactly the way they wanted. "We had never built a house before, and the ideas for this one were completely in our heads," they note. "Each room remained raw until we

Continued

The living room, right, has raised painted paneling on the walls and ceiling, a decorative feature that can be traced to medieval Nordic homes. Among the Danish antiques in the room are two stripped-pine settees fashioned from bedsteads, and a painted trunk dated 1837.

Designed for Copenhagen's Holmegaard glassworks by Per Lütken, one of Denmark's leading contemporary glass artists, the bowl above exhibits the simple, restrained lines typical of many Scandinavian hand-crafted pieces.

To create an intimate atmosphere in the dining room, right, no electric lights were installed; at night, dining is by candlelight. Ruddy-toned heart pine, used for flooring, wainscoting, and the floor-to-ceiling cupboard, contributes to the warm feeling of the room.

could decide how to finish it, and then we proceeded mainly on intuition." Little did they realize that it would be twelve years before the house was completed.

Many of the ideas for the design came from visits that the couple made to Denmark and Norway, where they were struck, in particular, by the beauty and simplicity of 15th-century architecture and interiors. Consequently, several of the rooms feature the exposed beams and raised panels typical of late-medieval Nordic houses. The painted decoration throughout the residence was also inspired by traditional Scandinavian craftsmanship. Some of the floral motifs that are hand-painted on the walls and ceilings, for example, were adapted from designs that characterize *rosemaling,* a type of decorative painting (often featuring flowers, leaves, and vines) that flourished in Norway from 1750 to 1850.

Other elements of the decor include materials

Continued

The open kitchen, above, often serves as a family gathering place. The wall paintings and the carving on the table and cabinets are adapted from traditional Scandinavian motifs.

The Scandinavian-style alcove bed above has built-in shelving at the head and storage drawers in the base. The painted decoration includes the initials of the child who sleeps here.

salvaged from old buildings that were being torn down. For instance, the heart pine boards used for flooring and paneling, and for the fireplace mantel in the living room, came from a two-hundred-year-old Connecticut textile mill. And the bricks that make up the kitchen floor were recycled from a 19th-century building in Colorado Springs. Not only do these additions bring warmth to the house, they also complement the Scandinavian look.

Beautiful handmade furniture also enhances the distinctive Nordic character of the house. In every room, Danish antiques—either passed down through the family or purchased during annual trips to Denmark—are combined with

new pieces that the homeowner designed himself. While not exact copies of Nordic furniture, many of the tables, chairs, and chests he crafted are painted or carved with typical Scandinavian motifs. Some of the pieces also feature the date when they were completed or the initials of a family member.

The elaborate Scandinavian-style alcove bed above, for example, was made for his daughter. Such spacesaving built-in beds, generally outfitted with doors or heavy curtains, have long been used in cold northern climates because they are efficient in conserving heat. Tucked in under the sloping ceiling, this charming "hideaway" has bifold doors fitted with hand-leaded glass.

The armoire at left was
painted to match the alcove
bed and, in addition to
initials, features the date
the piece was finished. Chip
carving enhances
the sides.

CARL LARSSON'S "ETT HEM"

Carl Larsson was an artist whose illustrations and paintings—done from the 1870s until his death at age sixty-five in 1919—brought him fame not only in his native Sweden but also throughout the world. Larsson's murals for the national museum and for the opera house, both in Stockholm, were highly acclaimed, as were his landscapes and portraits. Yet Larsson's most influential work was, perhaps, a series of twenty-six watercolors (six of which are shown at right) showing idyllic scenes and interiors of his country home in Sundborn, in central Sweden. Begun in 1894 and exhibited in Stockholm in 1897, the watercolors, collectively entitled *Ett Hem* (A Home), were published two years later in an album of the same name, which also included text by the artist.

Larsson claimed that it was his wife's idea that he start the watercolors to give him "something to do one summer when it rained for six weeks without let-up. . . ." Once he began the paintings, however, he intended them as documentation of their household. At the time, it was fashionable among middle-class

The interior of Carl Larsson's country cottage is the subject of these paintings from his album *Ett Hem.* At top, the parlor he called a "Lazy Nook"; at center, a bedroom used by his wife and their little girls; and at bottom, the artist's own bedroom, where he admittedly slept on a straw mattress "as soundly as a king on his catafalque."

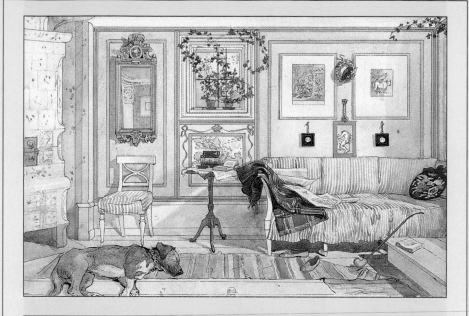

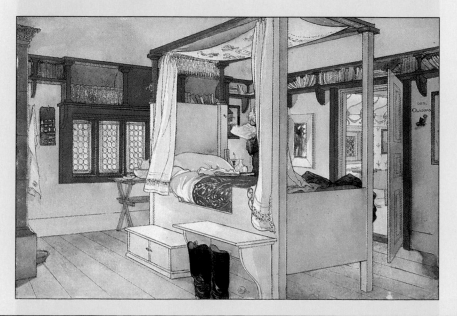

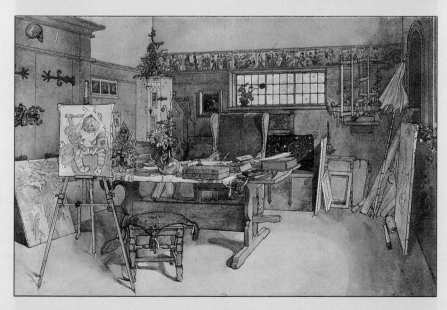

Swedish families to have their homes photographed and the photos bound into albums; Larsson wanted his album to be in watercolors instead.

Whether he also had bigger ideas in mind while he was doing the paintings is not known, but when *Ett Hem* was published, it is clear that the artist knew how the album might be used. As he suggested in the introduction: "It is not with the vain intention of showing merely how I live, but rather because I consider that I have been so sensible about all this that it might be worthwhile . . . as a guide . . . for many people who feel the need to fix up their homes in a nice way."

The "nice way" that Larsson advocated was a sunny, casual look very different from the heavy, overbearing decoration that had prevailed in Sweden for some time. People related to the artist's cheerful cottage—decorated with traditional Swedish folk crafts, pretty wallpapers and fabrics, and graceful neoclassical furniture—and readily responded to his ideas. As a result, *Ett Hem* was an instant success, and thousands of copies were sold.

An unusual leaded-glass window distinguishes the Larsson dining room, top. Another view of the dining room, center, offers a glimpse of "Old Anna," the family cook, at work. The artist's studio, bottom, features what Larsson called a "colossal old armchair," and a portrait in progress—possibly of his youngest daughter, Brita.

A Norwegian Collection

The cedar-plank residence above is located in western Wisconsin, a region where many Norwegians settled in the 19th century. The house was designed to accommodate a collection of Norwegian and Norwegian-immigrant furniture.

The owners of this Wisconsin residence, which was remodeled from a one-room schoolhouse built in the early 1900s, had two goals in mind when they began work on the house: it had to suit their collection of Norwegian and Norwegian-immigrant furnishings, and it had to be energy efficient. With its small windows, low ceilings, and thick wood planking—all of which help to conserve heat—the rustic building now evokes the simple cabins built by the Norwegian settlers who came to the region in the mid- to late 1800s.

The couple—one of whom is of Norwegian ancestry—became seriously interested in Norwegian antiques after a visit to Vesterheim, a Decorah, Iowa, museum committed to documenting the life and cultural traditions of the Norwegian immigrant in America. Since then, they have devoted themselves to studying and collecting the furnishings the settlers brought with them from their homeland, as well as those they made here.

While many of the pieces that were crafted in Norway—from chests to spoons—are decorated

Continued

Among the Norwegian-immigrant antiques at left is a pine drop-front secretary, which was crafted in Wisconsin around 1870. It is decorated with grain-painting and has a fretwork cornice, a typical feature on such pieces. The three-legged chair, or bandestol, also made in America, was originally designed to stand firmly on uneven packed-earth floors.

Two elaborately painted 19th-century chests from Telemark, a region of Norway noted for fine rosemaling, are found in the living room, right. Also from Norway is the chunky chair (known as a kubbestol), which was crafted from a single log. The two other chairs in the room—a pair made in this country (probably for a husband and wife) in the late 1800s—show a similar form.

The heddle above, a mechanism for guiding warp threads on a tape loom, was made in Norway in the early 19th century. The fine painting and carving is characteristic of traditional Nordic craftsmanship.

In Norway, carved birch
spoons like those above were
traditional courtship gifts,
presented by a prospective
groom to his betrothed. The
spoon on the left, made in
the late 19th century, has an
elaborate acanthus design
carved into the handle; the
one on the right, also from
that period, is decorated
with minute scratch
carving.

with carving or painting, almost none of those made in America were embellished in this way. This was because few of the craftsmen who practiced these arts in Norway chose to emigrate. Those who did leave their homeland found that settlers in the New World could not afford to hire them.

As one of the collectors observes, most Norwegian-American pieces are not recognizably Norwegian, and it therefore takes an expert eye to tell them apart from furniture made by other immigrants. There are notable exceptions, however, which can be seen in the couple's collection. The three-legged chair, known as a *bandestol*, and the rustic chair fashioned from a single log, called a *kubbestol*, while made in America, have been clearly linked to forms typically found in 18th- and 19th-century Norwegian households.

The cupboard above was built by an accomplished Norwegian-American woodworker, Lars Christenson, in the 1860s. Two eggbeaters and a fluted rolling pin sit on the counter.

The intricately carved hanging cupboard opposite is dated 1886 and inscribed with the names of a man and a woman, indicating that it was probably a wedding present. The chest beneath was made in Telemark, Norway, in 1785, and is decorated with elaborate rosemaling.

NORWEGIAN DECORATED TRUNKS

The carving on the c. 1700 trunk above shows the prophet Elijah being fed by angels and ravens, and, on one end, King David with his harp; fancy ironwork was used to reinforce the lid. On the 1837 trunk at right, from the district of Vest-Agder, carved arches frame simple floral designs done with *rosemaling*.

The wooden trunk, or *kiste*, was for centuries one of the most important furnishings in a Norwegian home. Such trunks are known to have been used by the Vikings, and they continued to be used—mainly for storing clothing and linens—in Nordic households until wardrobes and chests of drawers became common in the late 19th century. When Norwegians started emigrating to America in the 1820s, the sturdy trunks proved convenient for transporting their possessions.

The tradition of embellishing trunks is as old as the pieces themselves. The most elaborately decorated trunks, however, date from the mid-18th to the mid-19th centuries, when artistic craftsmanship developed and flourished under a prosperous economy. Although a trunk might be made by its owner, more often a carpenter would be hired to do the work. The carpenter might also enlist other professional craftsmen to add decorative carving, paint, or ironwork. Many of the most beautifully crafted trunks were those made for women's dowries.

The trunks shown here display some of the various decorative techniques that were used. One of the

The trunk above was painted by noted Telemark *rosemaler* Thomas Luraas, who added the year it was finished and the name of the owner; ornamental ironwork sets off the painted designs. The painted dower trunk at left features a stylized bride and groom and is inscribed with the name and birthdate of the bride-to-be.

most common was *rosemaling*—a type of folk painting based on floral motifs, which became popular in Norway around 1750. As this new art form spread, different Norwegian districts developed their own individual styles. For example, the *rosemaling* done in the district of Telemark usually features C-shaped leaves from which brightly colored flowers sprout in profusion. *Rose-*

maling from the Vest-Agder region features more symmetrical floral designs often rendered in dark colors.

Another artistic technique frequently used on trunks was carving. At first, designs were simply chipcarved, but as tools improved, the techniques became more elaborate. Three-dimensional carved biblical scenes were popular in the 17th and 18th centuries, and once *rosemaling*

caught on, carvers began to imitate its floral patterns.

Whether a trunk was carved or painted—or both—it generally was distinguished by some type of ironwork. Hinges and handles, keys and key plates, as well as the bands that girdled and reinforced a trunk, were often crafted with decorative outlines and incised surfaces to enhance the trunk's design.

Southwestern Style

*a distinctive regional look
inspired by the land*

T he style of the American Southwest is intimately linked to the land—to the colorful deserts, dramatic mountain ranges, and broad mesas that distinguish this remarkable region. It is a land where the architecture, both old and new, is one with the landscape; where ancient Indian pueblos, with their thick adobe walls and exposed log beams, still stand as they have for centuries. It is a land where the traditions of both the native Americans and the Spanish settlers who came to the region from Mexico beginning in the 1500s continue to be preserved.

The vibrant spirit of the Southwest is evident in the two houses on the following pages. One, a Spanish Colonial Revival cottage in southern California, makes bold use of bright colors to create a cheerful environment that suits an eclectic mix of colorful furnishings. The other, the apartment of a designer in Santa Fe, features collections of regional crafts and furniture. Here, Navajo rugs and Mexican weavings provide dramatic accents for rooms decorated with rustic New Mexican antiques.

A raised adobe fireplace is often used to warm this bedroom in Santa Fe.

A Colorful Cottage

With its red-clay roof tiles and stucco façade, this southern California cottage, built in 1921, is typical of the Spanish Colonial Revival architecture that reached the height of its popularity during the twenties. The couple who now own the residence have managed to preserve its Hispanic flavor while furnishing it with pieces collected in such diverse countries as Haiti, Guatemala, and the Philippines. Although the decor is eclectic, the house still has a unified feeling resulting from an imaginative use of color.

Both outdoors and in, the homeowners have combined the hues of sun, sea, sand, and sky typically seen on houses throughout Mexico and the desert Southwest. For the front of the house,

Continued

Above, a blue-painted walkway and a stately king palm draw attention to the colorful façade of this Spanish Colonial Revival cottage in Hollywood. The covered back porch, right, is warmed by a Mexican chiminea—or stove—and lit by a wrought-iron lantern similar to those used in Mexico.

they selected a rich shade of turquoise for the door and window trim and accented it with dusty rose. In the back of the house, lavender and a bolder pink were used to brighten the terrace area. These same colors, along with brilliant yellow and touches of terra-cotta, reappear on walls and furniture indoors.

In the open living and dining area, the couple wanted a weathered look similar to that of the painted and sun-bleached buildings of Baja and Oaxaca, in Mexico. To achieve it, they washed some of the painted surfaces with a light stain and sanded them to create a soft patina. Enhancing the effect, decorative borders in patterns resembling those often found on Southwestern baskets and other regional handcrafts were applied to the walls and fireplace surround.

Throughout the house, furniture and accessories provide additional color accents. In the children's bedroom the bright paint on a miniature

Continued

Furnishings gathered from around the world give an international feeling to the living and dining area,
where good luck talismans from the Philippines are mounted above all the doors. An early-1900s Afghan
rug and a contemporary Haitian banner, left, add bold color to the room, while turn-of-the-century
Philippine religious figures are used to decorate the fireplace mantel, above.

In the cheerful kitchen, above, small hand-painted and glazed tiles from Mexico are interspersed with larger terra-cotta floor tiles.

chair and table set from Mexico echoes the colors used on the walls. And in the living room, the colorful sofa cushion slipcovers—made from a handwoven Guatemalan fabric that is generally used for clothing—contrast dramatically with a boldly patterned rug from Afghanistan.

Many of the other furnishings, discovered at local flea markets, tag sales, and thrift shops, were added simply on whim. "Rather than wait to find exactly the right piece," the homeowners say, "we bought what readily came to hand." For instance, the four Spanish Baroque-style

chairs that serve as porch furniture are flea-market finds, given a new life with a coat of lavender paint. The French fruitwood armoire now used for storage in the living room was purchased because its style—not unlike that of a Spanish *trastero,* or freestanding cupboard— worked well with the other pieces that make up the room's decor. And the unusual living room fireplace grate was actually assembled by the homeowners themselves from two pieces of ironwork rescued from the truck of a Los Angeles junk dealer.

A miniature table and rush-seated chairs, bought at a roadside stand in Mexico, are colorful accents in the children's bedroom, above.

GROWING CACTI INDOORS

Natural accents for a Southwestern-style decor, cacti are among the easiest plants to grow indoors. Because they are succulents—plants that have adapted to their arid surroundings by developing water-retaining stems or leaves—cacti are extremely resilient and require little care; in fact, many can even tolerate neglect.

Small cacti like those shown here are ideal plants to raise indoors because they grow slowly and do not need much room. They will do best planted in a porous, quick-draining medium, such as a mixture of equal parts potting soil, coarse sand, and peat moss; be sure to use a pot with a drainage hole.

Cacti need lots of light and good ventilation, and will thrive on a sun-

ny windowsill. In warm weather, the plants will most likely require a thorough weekly watering and a light monthly feeding with a commercial fertilizer that contains nitrogen, phosphoric acid, and potash. In winter, cacti often go into a dormant pe-

riod lasting from two weeks to several months. During this resting stage they will produce no green tips or shoots and will need very little water or food. When the plants start to sprout again, it is time to resume feeding them.

Among the cacti above, all of which grow well indoors, are some that take their names from the way they look: Bunny Ears, Brain, Indian Corncob, and Old Man (with the white "beard").

In the Pueblo Style

While it is actually in a contemporary building, this apartment in Santa Fe has been designed with thick adobe walls, heavy wooden doors, and exposed log ceiling *vigas,* or beams, to recall the centuries-old pueblo architecture of the region. The rustic rooms provide a handsome setting for a collection of 19th- and 20th-century American Indian, New Mexican, and Mexican crafts and furnishings.

The weaver and textile designer who lives here has had a long-standing interest in handcrafts—particularly in textiles. Among the pieces she

Continued

Made in the town of Saltillo in northern Mexico, weavings like those above were originally worn over the shoulders on special occasions. Here, some have been carefully crafted into pillow covers.

In the cheerful room at left, Mexican textiles are used on a late-19th-century day bed. The Navajo rugs were woven in the early 1900s; the one with the figures depicts ye'ii, or holy people.

Exposed vigas, or beams,
are visible in the kitchen,
right, where terra-cotta floor
tiles and rustic furniture add
to the Southwestern feeling
of the room. The ceramic hen
on the worktable was made
in Mexico in the early 1900s
for the tourist trade.

has collected over the years are various early-20th-century Saltillo weavings, which are named for the town in northern Mexico where they were first made in the 1600s and continue to be crafted today. A number of these weavings, some with "rainbow" stripes and a central diamond, have been made into coverings for pillows, which are displayed on beds and built-in benches throughout the apartment. Used in combination with early-20th-century Navajo rugs, these textiles add color and drama to the spare white rooms.

An appreciation for the handmade also extends to the choice of other accessories, which include contemporary paintings and pottery made by local artists, as well as Indian baskets and cradleboards, and 19th-century Spanish *retablos*, or religious paintings done on wood panels. Perhaps the most striking piece on display, however, is the seven-foot-tall totem pole that dominates the master bedroom (overleaf).

In selecting furniture for the house, the owner wanted well-worn pieces that would suit the rustic decor. Nearly all the furnishings she purchased, including the New Mexican day bed in the master bedroom, the rush-seated Spanish country chairs in the dining room, and the scrub-top sugar pine table in the kitchen, are from the late 19th or early 20th century, and bear traces of their original paint.

The banco, *or built-in bench, in the dining room, above, is a traditional type of seating in adobe houses. Above it hang a turn-of-the-century ox yoke, and a Pueblo cradleboard with rawhide straps. The candlesticks are made from old branding irons.*

Native American artifacts distinguish the decor of the bedroom, right. The cradleboard above the bed is a Ute piece made in the 1920s; the totem pole was crafted in the late 19th century by members of the Nootka tribe in the Pacific Northwest.

The circa 1920 cottonwood
kachina doll above is one of
hundreds of such dolls used
by several Pueblo tribes to
educate children about
ancestral spirits. This doll is
thought to have been carved
by a member of the
Hopi tribe.

WEATHERING A CUPBOARD

A. Using smooth strokes, thinned paint is sponged onto the wood following the direction of the grain.

Weathering, a finishing technique in which paint is applied to a wood surface, then sanded to suggest wear, is well-suited to the sun-bleached look of furnishings associated with the Southwest. The directions below are for weathering a cupboard, but they can be applied to virtually any piece of unfinished furniture; pine is recommended because it absorbs the paint readily.

Aqua and cobalt were the choices for the two-color process shown here, but any combination will work. The sanding is done so that the first color shows through the second in rough patches; paint left in grooves will make dark accents. To keep the paint the right thickness, use a quarter of a can at a time, pouring and thinning more as needed. While an electric sander is suggested, you can also sand your piece by hand; step back as you work to check the effect.

MATERIALS

For a cupboard like the one opposite, which measures approximately 37 x 25 x 78 inches, you will need one quart each of the two paint colors you choose.

· Unfinished pine cupboard · Flat latex paint in two colors ·
· Small natural sea sponge · 2- to 4-inch soft-bristle paintbrush ·
· Containers for mixing paint · Fine sandpaper, 220 grit ·
· Electric sander · 1 pint amber paste wax · Soft cloth ·
· Masking tape · Paper towels ·

B. A paintbrush is used to apply a second paint color over the first in uneven patches.

DIRECTIONS

1. Remove the knobs from the cupboard, and cover the hinges with masking tape to protect them from paint splatters.

2. Pour ¼ can of the base-color paint into a container. Thin with water until the paint is the consistency of skim milk.

3. Dampen the sea sponge with water and squeeze it almost dry. Dip the sponge into the paint and squeeze out the excess. Following the direction of the wood grain, rub the paint into the wood (Illustration A), applying paint to all grooves and edges (it is fine if the paint is heavier in these areas). Continue until the entire cupboard is covered with paint, thinning new batches of paint as necessary. Let the paint dry thoroughly.

4. Thin the second paint color as in step 2. Dip the paintbrush into the paint and wipe off any excess on a paper towel until the brush is almost dry. Apply, following the grain of the wood and varying the density of the paint so that the first color shows through in uneven patches (Illustration B). Continuing in this manner, cover the whole piece with paint.

5. Using the electric sander, gradually sand down the top layer of paint (Illustration C), varying the pressure so that some patches are more heavily sanded than others. If you feel that you have removed too much paint, give these areas another wash using either of the two paint colors. If necessary, let the paint dry, and sand again.

6. For a rich patina, rub the entire piece with amber paste wax following the manufacturer's directions, and buff with a soft cloth.

7. Untape the hinges and replace the knobs.

C. Sanding away the second paint color in random areas enhances the weathered look of the piece.

Selected Reading

Borba, Nora, and Paula Panich. *The Desert Southwest*. New York: Bantam Books, Inc., 1987.

Boyce, Charles. *Dictionary of Furniture*. New York: Facts on File Publications, 1985.

Brittain, Judy, ed. *Terence Conran's Home Furnishings*. Boston: Little, Brown & Company, 1986.

Cliff, Stafford, and Suzanne Slesin. *French Style*. New York: Clarkson N. Potter, Inc., 1982.

Comstock, Helen, ed. *The Concise Encyclopedia of American Antiques*. New York: Hawthorn Books, n.d.

Cooke, Edward S., Jr., ed. *Upholstery in America from the Seventeenth Century to World War I*. New York: W.W. Norton & Company, 1987.

Dittrick, Mark, and Diane Kender Dittrick. *Decorative Hardware*. New York: Hearst Books, 1982.

Eastwood, Maud. *Antique Builders' Hardware: Knobs and Accessories*. Beaverton, Oreg.: Lithtex Printing, 1982.

Emmerling, Mary Ellisor. *Mary Emmerling's American Country West*. New York: Clarkson N. Potter, Inc., 1985.

Fabian, Monroe H. *The Pennsylvania-German Decorated Chest*. New York: Universe Books, 1978.

Foley, Mary Mix. *The American House*. New York: Harper & Row, 1980.

Garvan, Beatrice B. *The Pennsylvania-German Collection*. Philadelphia: The Philadelphia Museum of Art, 1982.

Gaynor, Elizabeth. *Finland Living Design*. New York: Rizzoli International Publications, Inc., 1984.

Gaynor, Elizabeth. *Scandinavia Living Design*. New York: Stewart, Tabori & Chang, Inc., 1987.

Gilbertson, Donald E., and James F. Richards, Jr. *A Treasury of Norwegian Folk Art in America*. Osseo, Wis.: Tin Chicken Antiques, and Callaway, Minn.: Maplelag, 1975.

Gilliatt, Mary. *English Country Style*. Boston: Little, Brown & Company, 1987.

Gilliatt, Mary. *The Complete Book of Home Design*. Boston: Little, Brown & Company, 1984.

Gray, Linda, with Jocasta Innes. *The Complete Book of Decorating Techniques*. Boston: Little, Brown & Company, 1986.

Grow, Lawrence. *Architectural Painting*. New York: Rizzoli, 1986.

Hornung, Clarence P. *Treasury of American Design: A Pictorial Survey of Popular Folk Arts*. New York: Harry N. Abrams, 1971.

Kauffman, Henry J. *Pennsylvania Dutch American Folk Art*. New York: Dover Publications, Inc., 1964.

Lynn, Catherine. *Wallpaper in America from the Seventeenth Century to World War I*. New York: W.W. Norton & Company, 1980.

Mather, Christine. *Santa Fe Style*. New York: Rizzoli International Publications, Inc., 1986.

Mayhew, Edgar deN., and Minor Myers, Jr. *A Documentary History of American Interiors from the Colonial Era to 1915*. New York: Charles Scribner's Sons, 1980.

Miller, Judith, and Martin Miller. *Period Details: A Sourcebook for House Restoration*. New York: Crown Publishers, 1987.

Montgomery, Florence M. *Textiles in America, 1650-1870*. New York: W.W. Norton & Company, 1984.

Moulin, Pierre, Pierre LeVec, and Linda Dannenberg. *Pierre Deux's French Country*. New York: Clarkson N. Potter, Inc., 1980.

Niesewand, Nonie. *The Home Style Book*. New York: Whitney Library of Design, 1984.

Nylander, Richard C. *Wallpapers for Historic Buildings: A Guide to Selecting Reproduction Wallpapers*. Washington, D.C.: Preservation Press, 1983.

O'Neil, Isabel. *The Art of the Painted Finish for Furniture and Decoration*. New York: William Morrow & Company, 1971.

Pettit, Florence H. *America's Printed and Painted Fabrics 1600-1900*. New York: Hastings House, 1970.

Pile, John F. *Interior Design*. New York: Harry N. Abrams, 1988.

Plath, Iona. *The Decorative Arts of Sweden*. New York: Dover Publications, Inc., 1966.

Saint Sauveur, Daphné de. *The French Touch*. Boston: Little, Brown and Company, 1988.

Seale, William. *Recreating the Historic House Interior*. Nashville: American Association for State and Local History, 1979.

Seebohm, Caroline, and Christopher Simon Sykes. *English Country*. New York: Clarkson N. Potter, Inc., 1987.

Seth, Sandra, and Laurel Seth. *Adobe! Homes and Interiors of Taos, Santa Fe and the Southwest*. Stamford, Conn.: Architectural Book Publishing Co., 1988.

Shea, John G. *The Pennsylvania Dutch and Their Furniture*. New York: Litton Educational Publishing, Inc., 1980.

Shipway, Verna Cook and Warren Shipway. *Mexican Interiors*. Stamford, Conn.: Architectural Book Publishing Co., Inc., 1962.

Slesin, Suzanne, and Stafford Cliff. *English Style*. New York: Clarkson N. Potter, Inc., 1984.

Stewart, Janice S. *The Folk Arts of Norway*. New York: Dover Publications, Inc., 1972.

Street-Porter, Tim. *Casa Mexicana*. New York: Stewart, Tabori & Chang, 1989.

Walker, Lester. *American Shelter*. Woodstock, N.Y.: The Overlook Press, 1981.

Wilson, José, and Arthur Leaman. *Decorating American Style*. Boston: New York Graphic Society, 1975.

Wilson, Kax. *A History of Textiles*. Boulder, Colo.: Westview Press, 1979.

Photography Credits

Cover, frontispiece, and pages 8, 16 (left), 20-35, 46-65, 70 (left), 75 (right), 76-77, 83 (right), 92-111, 122 (left), 126-127, 130-139, 142-147, 150, 158-167: Steven Mays. Pages 10-19 (except 16 left), 43 (right), 78-91 (except 83 right), 112-125 (except 117 right and 122 left): George Ross. Pages 36-43 (except 43 right): Mick Hales, courtesy of *House & Garden* © 1986.

Pages 44-45: Hulton-Deutsch Collection, London. Pages 66-75 (except 75 right): Jacques Dirand, courtesy of *House & Garden* © 1987. Pages 128-129: all photos (except bottom row center): courtesy of the Julius Sturgis Pretzel House, Lititz, PA; bottom row center: courtesy of The Bachman Company, Reading, PA. Pages 140-141: National Museum, Stockholm.

Page 148: Charles Langton, courtesy of Vesterheim, Norwegian-American Museum, Decorah, IA. Page 149: Charles Langton, courtesy of the Luther College Collection, Vesterheim, Norwegian-American Museum, Decorah, IA. Pages 152-157: Tim Street-Porter.

Prop Credits

The Editors would like to thank the following for their contributions as designers or consultants or for their courtesy in lending items for photography. Items not listed below are privately owned. **Page 8**: interior by Mary Meehan Interiors, Inc., NYC. **Page 16**: stirrup cup—Asprey, NYC. **Pages 20-21**: "Hunt Scene" dinner plates and oval serving dish, "Napoleon Ivy" bread and butter plate and vegetable dish—Wedgwood China, Wall, NJ; "Lismore" hand-cut crystal compote, hand-cut honey/jam jar and sugar bowl (holding jam)—Waterford Crystal, Wall, NJ; silver-plate chafing dish and round tray with handles—Oneida Silversmiths, Oneida, NY; squirrel/leaf dish—Mottahedeh & Co., NYC; tablecloth—Dampierre & Co., NYC; wallpaper, "Mary Cabot" #W2464, from American Collection—Stroheim & Romann, NYC. **Page 22**: "Hunt Scene" dinner plate, "Napoleon Ivy" bread and butter plate—Wedgwood China, Wall, NJ; "Lismore" hand-cut crystal glass, hand-cut crystal sugar dishes—Waterford Crystal, Wall, NJ. **Page 23**: "Lismore" hand-cut crystal compote—Waterford Crystal, Wall, NJ; squirrel/leaf dish—Mottahedeh & Co., NYC. **Pages 24-33**: interiors by Mary Meehan Interiors, Inc., NYC. **Pages 34-35**: chintz fabrics, top row, left to right:

"Cerise"—Rose Cumming Chintzes, NYC; "Ashley"—Lee Jofa, Inc., NYC; "Avril Print"—Lee Jofa, Inc.; "Ribbons & Pansies"—Rose Cumming Chintzes; middle row, left to right: "Corylus"—Osborne & Little, NYC; "Bagatelle"—Lee Jofa, Inc.; "Rose Medallion"—Rose Cumming Chintzes; "Milford"—Hinson & Company, NYC; bottom row, left to right: "Louise Elizabeth"—Lee Jofa, Inc.; "Blackberry"—Rose Cumming Chintzes; "Cerise"—Rose Cumming Chintzes; "Chelsea"—Sanderson, NYC; "Moiré Rose Print"—Lee Jofa, Inc. **Pages 36-43**: interiors by Ann LeConey of Ann LeConey, Inc., NYC. **Page 43**: Prattware—Houston Museum, Chattanooga, TN. **Page 46**: interior and trompe l'oeil painting by Richard Lowell Neas, NYC. **Page 55**: porcelain dog—Objects Plus, NYC. **Pages 56-57**: chairs courtesy of, top row, left to right: Howard Kaplan Antiques, NYC; Pierre Deux Antiques, NYC; Howard Kaplan Antiques; Howard Kaplan Antiques; Pierre Deux Antiques; Howard Kaplan Antiques; bottom row, left to right: T & K French Antiques, NYC; Howard Kaplan Antiques; Howard Kaplan Antiques; Pierre Deux Antiques; Howard Kaplan Antiques; T & K French Antiques. **Pages 58-63**: interiors by Lucille Danneman, The Yellow House, Cape Cod, MA;

architect—Gavin Speirs, Rosemont, PA. **Pages 64-65**: collection of vintage Quimper—Millicent Mali, RI; fabric—Souleiado, available exclusively through Pierre Deux, NYC. **Pages 66-75**: interiors and trompe l'oeil painting by Richard Lowell Neas, NYC. **Page 70**: faience plate—Frederick P. Victoria & Son, Inc., NYC. **Page 75**: engraving of bird—Ursus Prints, NYC. **Pages 76-77**: fabrics—Souleiado, available exclusively through Pierre Deux, NYC. **Pages 92-93**: Lehnware collection courtesy of Sandra H. Lane, Sandy Lane Antiques, Bowmansville, PA. **Pages 110-111**: jacquard coverlets—Dr. and Mrs. Donald M. Herr. **Page 135**: blue bowl designed by Per Lütken, Copenhagen, available through Georg Jensen, NYC. **Pages 150, 160-165**: interiors by Chris O'Connell of Spider Woman Designs, Santa Fe, NM. **Page 165**: kachina doll—Common Ground, NYC. **Pages 166-167**: "Country Entertainment Unit" #9058—Mastercraft/S.J. Bailey & Sons, Inc., Clarks Summit, PA; decorative treatment by Dan Sevigny, Brooklyn, NY; rugs, chair, shelf, candle stands, retablo—ABC Carpet & Home, NYC; glass urns—Pottery Barn, NYC.

Index

A

adobe
  fireplace, 151
  walls, 161
alcove bed, 131, 138
apothecary chest, 119
appliquéd quilts, 90, 124
armchairs
  caned, 24
  chintz, 9
  ladder-back, 48
  leather, 100
  oversize, 27
armoire, 139, 157
art nouveau style, 54
Arts and Crafts style, 30
artwork
  botanical prints, 31, 40
  sporting, 12, 17, 40
  see also carvings; engravings;
    paintings

B

back-stool, 98
banco, 163
bandestol, 143, 147
bank house, 113, 115-116
barns
  pole, 10
  stone, 10, 18
baskets, 60
  coiled rye, 109, 125
  splint-woven, 109, 119
bed
  alcove, 131, 138
  dark wood, 32
  day, 48, 163
  marriage, 87
  rope, 107
  turned posts, 124
bedrooms
  English country, 30, 31, 32, 40, 42,
    73
  French country, 54, 62, 74
  Pennsylvania-German, 105, 107,
    123, 124
  Scandinavian, 138
  Southwestern, 151, 155-156, 157,
    164

bench, built-in (*banco*), 163
bergère, 74
bird
  carvings, 90, 123
  distilfink, 110
  engravings, 75
  painted decoration, 90
  tree, 122, 123
blanket chests, 87, 121, 123
blueberry-ginger scones (recipe), 23
botanical prints, 31, 40
boxes
  brides', 83
  candlebox, 52
  hat, 40
breakfront, faux-bamboo, 27
brides' boxes, 83
Brosey, John, 104
butter prints, 119

C

cacti, growing indoors, 158-159
cake, lemon-almond pound (recipe), 23
candlebox, 52
candlesticks, iron, 163
canister, smoke-decorated, 118
carpets. *see* rugs
carriage, antique, 10
  artwork, 15
  Park Drag, 18
carving(s)
  birds, 90, 123
  chip carving, 139
  gouge carving, 97, 107, 115
  scratch carving, 146
  spoons, 146
  trunk (*kiste*), 148, 149
ceilings
  exposed beam (*viga*), 161, 162
  molded plaster, 24, 27
  painted wood, 51
  raised paneling, 134, 137
  whitewash, 48
chairs
  bandestol, 143, 147
  bergère, 74
  chaise à capucine, 56-57
  chaise à dossier en médaillon, 74
  club, 30

French, 48, 51, 56-57, 60, 68, 74
  kubbestol, 144, 147
  Moravian, 98, 105, 107
  plank (back-stools), 98
  Queen Anne, 13
  rocker, ladder-back, 54
  rush-seated, 56-57, 60, 157, 163
  see also armchairs
chaise, English, 30
chaise à capucine, 56-57
chaise à dossier en médaillon, 74
chandelier, trompe l'oeil, 67
Chartwell Manor, 44
chests
  apothecary, 119
  blanket, 87, 121, 123
  rosemaling, 131, 144, 147
  see also trunk
china
  Spode stone, 27
  see also porcelain
Chinese porcelain, 27, 29
chintz, 9, 39, 42
  history, 34
  quilt, 123
chip carving, 139
Chippendale style, 13, 29
Christenson, Lars, 147
clocks, tall-case, 48, 82
clothing, hunting, 17
Colonial Revival architecture, Spanish,
  152, 155-157
cookware, 53, 54, 60
  see also kitchen utensils
corner cupboards, 97, 124
cotton
  damask, 39
  Indian (*indienne*), 76
coverlets, Pennsylvania-German, 104
  history, 110
country house, English, history, 44-
  45
cradleboard, 163, 164
cupboards
  corner, 97, 124
  dresser, 116
  floor-to-ceiling, 136
  French, 71
  grain-painted, 79, 121

hanging, 103, 147
by Lars Christenson, 147
lattice-door, 60
painted decoration, 84
weathering (project), 166-167
curtains, 54, 68, 74

D

damask, 39, 54
Danish style, mountain house decor in,
132-133, 137-138
decorative painting. *see* painted
decoration
delftware, 67, 74
De Turk, Philip, 105
dining rooms
English country, 13, 29
French country, 51, 52
Pennsylvania-German, 84, 103, 116
Scandinavian, 136
Southwestern, 155, 163
distilfink, 110
dogs
papier-mâché, 71
portrait, 40
dolls, Native American (kachina), 165
doors
French, 24
painted decoration, 40
drawing room, English country, 12
Dry pottery works, 117
dyes, analine, 34

E

eagle motif, 110
earthenware. *see* pottery
eggs, dilled, scrambled with smoked
salmon (recipe), 22
Empire style, 32
English country house, history, 44-45
English country style, 9
chintz in, 9, 34-35
in farmhouse, 10, 12-13, 17-18
floral theme, 36-37, 39-40
in Tudor-style house, 24, 29-31
engravings
carriage, 12, 17
flora and fauna, 75
Ett Hem (Carl Larsson), 140-141

F

fabric
block-printed, 76
checked pattern, 71, 73
damask, 39, 54
floral and striped pattern, 73
French, 51, 59, 68, 71, 74, 76
Guatemalan, 156
indienne (Indian cotton), 76
linen (French), 68, 71, 74
Provençal, 51, 59
silk, 54
small-print, 54
tapestry-like, 27
see also chintz
faience, 59, 65, 70, 71, 74
fireplace
adobe, 151
with folding doors, 116, 118
Franklin, 98
kitchen, 100, 116, 118
walk-in, 52, 53
see also mantelpiece
floors
brick, 100, 138
heart pine, 136, 138
marbleized pattern, 37
terra-cotta tile, 156, 162
trompe l'oeil, 71, 74
pickled, 39
floral motif, 73
fabric, 29, 32, 60. *see also* chintz
flower and dove, 62
in garden decor, 36-37, 39-40
rosemaling, 131, 137, 147, 148,
149
tulip, 83, 110, 121
wallpaper, 29, 54
foods
hunt breakfast (recipes), 21-23
pretzel bakeries, 128-129
pretzels, soft (recipe), 126-127
shoofly pie, 117
fraktur, 79, 84, 87, 90, 114, 122
Franklin fireplace, 98
French country style, 47
fabrics, 51, 59, 68, 71, 74, 76
farmhouse, 67, 71, 73-74
indienne (Indian cotton), 76

Old-World, 48, 51-52, 54
Quimper pottery, 65
rush-seated chair (*chaise à
capucine*), 56-57
seaside house, 59-60
friendship quilts, 107

G

ginger jars, Chinese, 29
glass
blown, 87
leaded, 24, 138, 141
Scandinavian contemporary, 135
Vaseline, 33
gouge carving, 97, 107, 115
grain-painting, 79, 92, 105, 121,
143
Grandmother's Flower Garden pattern quilt, 42

H

hat boxes, 40
heddle, 145
Herr, David, 122
Hoff, George, 82
hooked rugs, 89, 114
horses
bronze, 15
figurine, 73
sporting art, 17
hunt breakfast (recipes), 21-23
hunt desk, 15
hunting box, English style, 10, 12-13,
17-18
hunting memorabilia, 15, 53
clothing, 17
horn, 52
stirrup cup, 16
hunt room, 13, 15
hutch, Pennsylvania-German, 52

I

indienne (Indian cotton), 76
ironstone, 116
ironwork, 54, 102, 149, 152, 163

J

jacquard coverlets, 110
jugs, Prattware, 43

K

kachina dolls, 165
kettle, copper, 53
kitchens
    French country, 60
    Pennsylvania-German, 94, 96, 116, 117, 118, 119
    Scandinavian, 137
    Southwestern, 156, 162
kitchen utensils, 53, 54, 102, 116, 147
kubbestol, 144, 147

L

lamps, Staffordshire figurine, 42, 73
lanterns, 52, 152
Larsson, Carl, 140-141
Lawton (J. A.) coachworks, 18
Lehn, Joseph, 92
Lehnware, 92
lemon-almond pound cake (recipe), 23
Levaillant, François, 75
library, English country, 24
linen, French, 68, 71, 74
living room
    English country, 27, 30-31, 39
    French country, 48, 68
    Pennsylvania-German, 82
    Scandinavian, 134
    Southwestern, 155
    see also drawing room; parlor; sitting room
Luraas, Thomas, 149
Lütken, Per, 135

M

majolica, 71
mantelpiece
    heart pine, 138
    marbleized, 74
    gouge-carved, 115
    painted decoration, 54
    paneled, 68
    see also fireplace
marbleized finish, 37, 40, 74
mich wisch, 97
Moravian chairs, 98, 105, 107
Morning Glory pattern ironstone, 116

N

Native American artifacts, 163, 164, 165
Natural History of African Birds, 75
Navajo rugs, 161, 163
needlepoint pillows, 31
Norwegian style
    cabin decor, 142, 147
    rosemaling, 131, 137, 144, 147, 148, 149
    trunk (*kiste*), 148-149

O

Oriental rugs, 27
Otto, Henrich, 84, 90, 122

P

painted decoration, 39, 40, 54, 62, 84, 87, 90, 132
    grain-painting, 79, 92, 105, 121, 143
    marbleizing, 37, 40, 74
    pickling, 39
    rosemaling, 131, 137, 144, 147, 148, 149
    sponge-painting, 67, 74
    trompe l'oeil, 40, 47, 67, 70, 71, 74
    weathering, 155, (project) 166-167
paintings
    ancestral portraits, 44
    canine portraits, 40
    by Carl Larsson, 140-141
    in fraktur tradition, 122
    landscape, 54
    religious (*retablos*), 163
    sporting, 17
paneling
    heart pine, 138
    raised painted, 134, 137
papier-mâché dog, 71
Park Drag carriage, 18
parlor, Pennsylvania-German, 115
Pennsylvania-German, 79
    collecting crafts and furnishings, 80-81, 84, 87, 104-105, 112-113
    jacquard coverlets, 110
    Lehnware, 92
    log and stone farmstead, 94-95, 98, 100, 103, 104-105, 107

pretzel bakeries, 128-129
pretzels, soft (recipe), 126-127
stone farmstead, 112-113, 115-116, 121, 123
pewter inlay, 98, 107
pickled finish, 39
pie plate, redware, 117
pillows
    hand-painted, 40
    needlepoint, 31
    woven, 161
porcelain, 31
    Chinese, 27, 29
    soft-paste, 55
    see also china
porch
    English country, 36
    Southwestern, 152
Portland Cutter sleigh, 18
potatoes, pan-fried, with scallions (recipe), 22
pottery
    delftware, 67, 74
    faience, 59, 65, 70, 71, 74
    glazed, 60
    ironstone, 116
    majolica, 71
    Mexican, 162, 163
    Prattware, 143
    Quimper, 65
    redware, 117, 121
    spatterware, 97
    Staffordshire, 42, 71, 73
    stoneware, 119
pound cake, lemon-almond (recipe), 23
Pratt, William, 43
Prattware, 43
pressed-glass compote, 33
pretzels
    bakeries, 128-129
    soft (recipe), 126-127
punched decoration, 101

Q

Queen Anne style, 13
quilting template, 114
quilts, 32, 89
    appliquéd, 90, 124

chintz, 123
friendship, 107
Grandmother's Flower Garden, 42
Rose of Sharon, 124
Quimper pottery, 65

R

rag rug, 114
redware, 117, 121
Regency style, 24, 29, 30
retablos, 163
rocker, ladder-back, 54
rocking horse, 121
roof, cedar-shake, 133
rope bed, 107
rosemaling, 131, 137, 144, 147, 148,
    149
Rose of Sharon quilt, 124
rugs
    Afghanistan, 156
    hooked, 89, 114
    Navajo, 161, 163
    Oriental, 27
    rag, 114
rush-seated chairs, 56-57, 60, 157,
    163

S

Saltillo weavings, 163
Scandinavian style, 131
    of Carl Larsson, 140-141
    Danish mountain house, 132-133,
        137-138
    Norwegian cabin, 142, 147
    rosemaling, 131, 137, 144, 147,
        148, 149
    trunk (*kiste*), 148-149
schrank, 79, 87, 98, 100, 105
schtubb (stove room), 98, 100, 121,
    123
scones, blueberry-ginger (recipe), 23
scrambled eggs, dilled, with smoked
    salmon (recipe), 22
scratch carving, 146
secretary
    drop-front, 143
    pine, 39
settee, stripped-pine, 134

shoofly pie, 117
sideboard, 13, 15, 29
Simmons, "Schtochschnitzler," 123
sitting room, English country, 40
slaw cutter, 116
sleighs, antique, 10
    Portland Cutter, 18
smoke decoration, 118
smokehouse, 95
soft-paste porcelain, 55
Southwestern style, 151, 158-159
    collecting crafts and furnishings, 161,
        163
    Colonial Revival cottage, 152,
        155 157
    weathering technique, 155, (project)
        166-167
spatterware, 97
Spode stone china, 27
sponge-painting, 67, 74
spoons
    carved, 146
    stuffing, 52
sporting art, 12, 17, 40
Staffordshire, 42, 71, 73
stirrup cup, 16
stoneware, 119
stoves, 123, 152
stove room (*schtubb*), 98, 100, 121,
    123
Stubbs, George, 40
Sturgis pretzel bakery, 128, 129
Swedish style, of Carl Larsson, 140-
    141

T

tables
    Chippendale, 29
    Empire, 32
    farm, 51, 52, 59
    French, 51, 60, 68
    hunt desk, 15
    miniature, 157
    Queen Anne, 13
    refectory, 15
    Regency, 24, 30
    scrub-top pine, 163
    trestle, 116

tableware
    Vaseline glass, 33
    see also china; porcelain; pottery
Telemark *rosemaling*, 131, 144, 147,
    149
textiles. *see* fabric; pillows; quilts; rugs;
    weavings
tiles
    marbleized pattern, 37
    Mexican, 156
    trompe l'oeil, 71
tinware, Pennsylvania-German, 84, 101
tomatoes, grilled basil (recipe), 22
tools, 52, 53, 59
trestle table, 116
trompe l'oeil, 40, 47, 67, 70, 71, 74
trunk (*kiste*), Norwegian, 134, 148-149
Tudor-style architecture, 24, 29-31

V

Vaseline glass, 33
Vest-Agder *rosemaling*, 148, 149
vigas, 161, 162

W

walls
    adobe, 161
    raised paneling, 134, 137
    sponge-painted, 67, 74
    trompe l'oeil, 47, 74
    weathered, 155
    whitewashed, 24, 48, 60, 109
wallpaper, 29, 42, 51, 54
weathering, 155, (project) 166-167
weavings, 110, 161, 163
whitewash, 24, 48, 60, 109
wicker furniture, 36, 54
windows
    diamond-paned, 24
    leaded-glass, 24, 138, 141
winged head, Pennsylvania-German,
    103
woodenware
    Lehnware, 92
    see also carvings

Acknowledgments

Our thanks to Hilary and Michael Anderson, Lucille Danneman, Nancy and Don Gilbertson, June and Robert Holman, Charles Langton, Ann LeConey, Mary Meehan, Richard Lowell Neas, Marion Nelson, Chris O'Connell and the staff of Spider Woman Designs, Dr. Donald J. Rosato and Judy Rosato, Joanne and Donald Stoughton, Clyde Tshudy, and Anne Vitte and Terry Morse for their help on this book.

First printing
Published simultaneously in Canada
School and library distribution by Silver Burdett Company,
Morristown, New Jersey

TIME-LIFE is a trademark of Time Incorporated U.S.A.

Production by Giga Communications, Inc.
Printed in U.S.A.

Library of Congress Cataloging-in-Publication Data

Country traditions
p. cm. — (American country)
Includes index.
ISBN 0-8094-7058-6 — ISBN 0-8094-7059-4 (lib. bdg.)
1. Country homes—United States—Themes, motives.
2. Architecture, Domestic—United States—Foreign influences.
3. Decoration and ornament, Rustic—United States—Themes, motives.
4. Interior decoration—United States—Foreign influences.
I. Time-Life Books. II. Series.
NA7561.C7   1990   728'.37'0973—dc20   90-11003
CIP

American Country was created by Rebus, Inc., and published by Time-Life Books.

REBUS, INC.

Publisher: RODNEY FRIEDMAN • Editor: MARYA DALRYMPLE
Executive Editor: RACHEL D. CARLEY • Managing Editor: BRENDA SAVARD • Consulting Editor: CHARLES L. MEE, JR.
Copy Editor: ALEXA RIPLEY BARRE • Writer: ROSEMARY G. RENNICKE
Design Editors: NANCY MERNIT, CATHRYN SCHWING
Test Kitchen Director: GRACE YOUNG • Editor, The Country Letter: BONNIE J. SLOTNICK
Contributing Editors: LEE CUTRONE, ANNE MOFFAT
Indexer: MARILYN FLAIG

Art Director: JUDITH HENRY • Associate Art Director: SARA REYNOLDS
Designers: AMY BERNIKER, TIMOTHY JEFFS
Photographer: STEVEN MAYS • Photo Editor: SUE ISRAEL
Photo Assistant: ROB WHITCOMB • Freelance Photographer: GEORGE ROSS
Freelance Photo Stylists: VALORIE FISHER, DEE SHAPIRO • Set Carpenter: MARCOS SORENSEN

Series Consultants: BOB CAHN, HELAINE W. FENDELMAN, LINDA C. FRANKLIN, GLORIA GALE,
KATHLEEN EAGEN JOHNSON, JUNE SPRIGG, CLAIRE WHITCOMB

Time-Life Books Inc. is a wholly owned subsidiary of THE TIME INC. BOOK COMPANY.

President and Chief Executive Officer: KELSO F. SUTTON
President, Time Inc. Books Direct: CHRISTOPHER T. LINEN

TIME-LIFE BOOKS INC.

Editor: GEORGE CONSTABLE
Director of Design: LOUIS KLEIN • Director of Editorial Resources: PHYLLIS K. WISE
Director of Photography and Research: JOHN CONRAD WEISER

President: JOHN M. FAHEY JR.
Senior Vice Presidents: ROBERT M. DeSENA, PAUL R. STEWART, CURTIS G. VIEBRANZ, JOSEPH J. WARD
Vice Presidents: STEPHEN L. BAIR, BONITA L. BOEZEMAN, MARY P. DONOHOE, STEPHEN L. GOLDSTEIN,
ANDREW P. KAPLAN, TREVOR LUNN, SUSAN J. MARUYAMA, ROBERT H. SMITH
New Product Development: TREVOR LUNN, DONIA ANN STEELE
Supervisor of Quality Control: JAMES KING

Publisher: JOSEPH J. WARD

For information about any Time-Life book please call 1-800-621-7026, or write:
Reader Information, Time-Life Customer Service
P.O. Box C-32068, Richmond, Virginia 23261-2068

Time-Life Books Inc. offers a wide range of fine recordings, including a Rock 'n' Roll Era series.
For subscription information, call 1-800-621-7026, or write TIME-LIFE MUSIC,
P.O. Box C-32068, Richmond, Virginia 23261-2068.